BAKING

SPICE MIXES

SPICES

STONE EDGE FARM

KITCHEN LARDER COOKBOOK

STONE EDGE FARM
KITCHEN LARDER COOKBOOK

SEASONAL RECIPES FOR PANTRY AND TABLE

JOHN McREYNOLDS, MIKE EMANUEL, AND FIORELLA BUTRON

PHOTOGRAPHS BY LESLIE SOPHIA LINDELL

RIZZOLI
NEW YORK

New York · Paris · London · Milan

CONTENTS

Three cooks and a gardener: (left to right) John McReynolds,
Colby Eierman, Fiorella Butron, and Mike Emanuel

THREE COOKS AND A GARDENER

Seven years ago, on a particularly hot midsummer day, Colby Eierman walked into my life. I was standing in the kitchen at Ramekins Cooking School in Sonoma, California, getting ready to teach a class. Colby was carrying a big box of beautiful vegetables, with a bit of a swagger and an impish grin under his wide-brimmed hat. He looked the part of the new American farmer: tall, tan, and confident, wearing slightly soiled jeans and the requisite short-sleeved plaid shirt. We shook hands and I immediately realized I had found the new gardener for Stone Edge Farm. At least, I hoped so.

A certified master gardener, Colby carried an impressive résumé, including stints at the Napa culinary center Copia, the highly regarded Benziger Winery in Sonoma Valley and Clif Family Winery in Napa Valley, and most recently Ramekins. I casually mentioned that we were looking for a gardener both for our produce needs and for the local restaurants we were then supplying. I asked if he might be interested. The very next day, after a tour of our gardens and a meeting with the owner of Stone Edge Farm, Mac McQuown, Colby was on board.

Colby had recently published a book, *Fruit Trees in Small Spaces*, that included a chapter written by a buddy, the chef Mike Emanuel. That chapter, "A Bounty of Seasonal Fruit Recipes," is filled with Mike's inventive recipes for quince paste, peach leaf wine, and pears poached in red wine. Mike, I learned, had worked for several years at Chez Panisse and cooked for a client as a private chef. A few months later, I hosted a book-signing event for Colby at the farm and finally got to meet Mike.

He appeared at the doorway with slightly tousled hair and a graying goatee, toting a large leather bag over his shoulder. I recognized him as a kindred spirit as we hugged each other in greeting. You know the guy who likes to be in the middle of the action, talking, laughing, hugging, sharing? That's Mike. He also happens to be a passionate and knowledgeable cook whose unflagging curiosity about food has no limits. I have always been that chef who never tires of talking about, exploring, and learning about food. Some call it obsession—my wife and daughter, for instance. I call it passion. In Mike I found someone with that same drive and desire about cooking. At the time, I cooked for Mac and Leslie McQuown on the weekends and attempted to help get our fledgling Stone Edge Farm Winery off the ground during the week.

For several years, Mike would pop up to Sonoma every once in a while and hang out with Colby or visit with me in my kitchen, a former garage next to the Cabernet Sauvignon vineyard. I was writing the *Stone Edge Farm Cookbook* (published in 2013), and the winery was finding its footing and direction. As the frequency and size of winery events at Stone Edge Farm grew, the garage kitchen and our dining room in a converted shed, while charming, were not ideal. Mac and Leslie found a restaurant for sale in downtown Sonoma that was destined to be our new event and dining space. Two years of renovation and Edge became our new home. My focus shifted to the new enterprise. Mike joined us, cooking half-time for Mac and Leslie and working with me the rest of the time. He brought the lineage of Chez Panisse and his own wealth of experience and creativity to Edge. After more than thirty years in countless kitchens, for the first time I had a chef to collaborate with and learn from.

With Mike on the scene, we now had a pipeline to the network of ex-Chez Panisse cooks who dot the Bay Area, many of whom work as freelance caterers and private chefs. Mike seemed to know everyone in the food world, especially in Napa. Four years ago when we needed extra help for an event, he reeled in his friend Fiorella Butron, a private chef from Peru who moon-lighted occasionally for other chefs and caterers. Luckily, she had a free night away from her regular gig, and we three cooked together for the first time.

Standing just five feet two inches, with a flowing mane of wavy chestnut hair and a fiery personality, Fiorella is all business . . . until you get to know her. That first night, she revealed her deep knowledge of cookery and technique, and modeled for Mike and me a gift for impeccable cleanliness and organization. Channeling her Peruvian, Palestinian, and Genoese ancestors, she goes deep into every aspect of food and life. Fiorella describes herself as a *bruja*, or "witch"—the good kind. She brews healing elixirs and tinctures and is the mistress of ferments. Fiorella became a frequent fixture in the kitchen whenever she was able to get away from other commitments. Sensing that we could lose this talented chef, we offered her a full-time job that, happily for us, she accepted.

Mike, Fiorella, and I have a silent partner in the kitchen, and he is Mac McQuown. Mac rarely ventures into our fast-paced domain that buzzes with constant banter, but his vision inspires us as much as the exquisite produce Colby delivers.

Mac grew up on a farm in Illinois and was introduced by his uncle to sustainable farming. He became an appreciator and then a collector of fine wines, always aware of the harmony between wine and food. He matched this sophisticated grasp of the relationship between the cellar and the kitchen with an environmental ethos rooted in his childhood experience. Stone Edge Farm collects solar energy capable of manufacturing enough hydrogen to power the entire property. Its carbon impact is negative and it is not reliant on the power grid. We don't waste natural resources like sunshine, and we preserve what produce we can't use as soon as it is harvested. The wine grapes grown in our vineyard, preserved for the most part in our winery but also in our kitchen, are a quintessential example of a food given an extended life. In the winery, grapes are vinified to last for years and to improve, of course, in a collector's cellar. We think of these wines as supreme larder ingredients, cooking with them and pairing them with dishes on our menus at Edge.

I have found that life is not usually a straight line but is more like a painting that takes a lifetime to complete, with many surprises—good, bad, and indifferent—along the way. The synergy that Mike, Fiorella, and I have created in the kitchen, with Colby in the garden, illustrates what can happen when opportunity and inspiration intersect. —*John McReynolds, Culinary Director*

WELCOME TO EDGE

Welcome to Edge, Stone Edge Farm's turn-of-the-century Victorian home in downtown Sonoma, California. Framed by two ancient Sevillano olive trees, it is painted in subtle shades of beige, raw umber, and gray and surrounded by a low boxwood hedge, with a simple metal gate bearing our Vine of Life logo in cast bronze. Edge is part restaurant, part private club, and part event space. But really, it feels more like a home—comfortable and intimate, with modern artwork and contemporary furnishings and design. Not to forget our Sonoma past, painted portraits of prominent settlers hang on one wall and an original stained and tattered California Republic Bear Flag still flies under a glass frame.

It is late afternoon and we are preparing the dining room for the evening's guests. The flower arrangements have been delivered, the place settings checked one last time, and the wineglasses polished to a brilliant shine. Unlike the often stressful and chaotic pace of a fine-dining restaurant, Edge is a sanctuary of calm. All of us who work here have the single vision of serving our guests the best from our farm and vineyards in a relaxed and unhurried atmosphere.

The kitchen still has the prep-time music blaring at full volume, but soon it will switch to something more restrained for the dinner hour. The chefs are a mix of backgrounds and cooking styles—firmly rooted in the classics but not afraid to push some boundaries and take inspiration from all continents, disciplines, and perspectives. Their real inspiration, however, comes from the gardens at Stone Edge Farm, where literally hundreds of different vegetable varieties are grown. The weekly deliveries from the farm create a happy buzz among the chefs, with one idea after another spilling out for the week's menus. Sometimes the kitchen at Edge seems more like a culinary laboratory, especially with fermentations bubbling, dehydrators humming, and ideas flying around.

Okay, we have the place, the talent, and the ingredients. What else? The heart and soul of Stone Edge Farm is the winery and the wines we make. Each is the full expression of every vineyard, every block, and every vine. The wines inspire our chefs to create food that enhances the dining and wine-drinking experience by constantly fine-tuning the dishes. We frequently taste the wines together to revisit in our minds the flavor profiles and offer feedback about the pairings, all with a true sense of collaboration. Just to keep things interesting, we also serve French wines from Bordeaux so our guests can experience the best of the Old World along with the New World.

Imagine a restaurant that grows its own grapes and makes its own wine, farms its own vegetables, presses its own olive oil, and bakes its own bread. That's Edge. The passion and care our gardener and his staff put into growing and picking our produce is matched by the passion and care we show to our guests. We are inspired to treat every visitor with the same care that is taken to nurture a single vine into a bottle of our wine. We hope you will visit, and experience the hospitality of Edge for yourself. —*Larry Nadeau, Director of Dining and Private Events*

THE KITCHEN LARDER

BAKING

SPICE MIXES

SPICES

The Kitchen Larder

We run a frugal kitchen. To us, frugality does not mean going without, or scrimping, or withholding generosity. Rather, our philosophy is that we have a sacred duty as cooks not to be wasteful. Nothing goes in the garbage. Even scraps and peels become compost that will nourish another season's vegetables.

How can we possibly use all the boxes of tomatoes that Colby, our director of gardens, has just brought into the kitchen? Even if we put fresh tomatoes on every menu, it's still too many. Preserving produce during its abundant season means both being frugal as we define it and, even more importantly, using it to add extra flavor and nuance to our cooking. In preparing an ingredient for the larder, we are honoring it and also making it available for the coming year.

Our Mediterranean climate, coupled with the healthy, pesticide-free soils at Stone Edge Farm, translates to enviable growing conditions in our vineyards, orchard, and garden. Here in Sonoma Valley, so many edible plants grow vigorously with little encouragement that locals describe them as growing like weeds. When the abundance of fruits and vegetables coming from the farm occasionally overwhelms us, we still appreciate it, and we keep the wheels of preservation turning.

Roughly 50 percent of all produce grown in the United States is thrown away—not eaten, not preserved, and not even composted. We don't believe in wasting food, and often the preserved food tastes even better than the original version. We preserve it for our larder out of respect for the farmer, who nurtured the plant from seed to harvest. We do it because we acknowledge that it is important to preserve the limited resources of our earth.

We cook from the whole kitchen. By this I mean we draw heavily from the larder, a word sometimes associated with an earlier generation or an era when kitchens didn't have refrigerators. A larder contains foodstuffs that have been transformed into a new version of themselves for long-term storage, whether through fermentation, drying, canning, or salting. The term *larder* has its origins in the old Anglo-French word for the cool room where meats were cured and stored. Our meat larder includes prosciutto, pancetta, and jars of duck confit. All in all, the larder represents the heart and soul of our kitchen. It reflects our philosophy that the farmer, the cook, and the diner are interconnected, and strengthens our commitment to the health of the natural world.

Cabbage, cucumbers, and other vegetables take on an altogether new flavor through the alchemy of lacto-fermentation. Through this metabolic process, they retain healthful vitamins and enzymes to make them more digestible. Familiar favorites such as kimchi, dill pickles, and sauerkraut all have that savory tang we associate with fermented vegetables, and every culture has its own spin on the process. As Fiorella introduced us to her fermentation repertoire, we began to explore and expand the limits of what we could ferment. Mike introduced us to the process of dehydrating fermented red pepper paste into an intense tangy powder. We also took inspiration from what other chefs are doing, especially the techniques described by Cortney Burns and Nicolaus Balla in the *Bar Tartine* cookbook and Sandor Katz in *The Art of Fermentation*, two essential references in the world of fermentation.

Because Stone Edge Farm is a winery, I have been asked if wine is a larder item. It certainly is! Fermentation of grapes began at the dawn of human civilization and has been a continuous part of culture anywhere wine grapes grow. Our distant ancestors discovered that fresh grape juice becomes safe to drink and store after undergoing fermentation. It also improves with age. Wine is not limited to its role as a beverage, however. It claims an essential place in the kitchen at Edge.

Before Mike and Fiorella came on board, when I wasn't at the grill, stove, or oven I was content to preserve lemons, dehydrate vegetables, cure olives, make fresh herb oils, and ferment wine vinegars. I had also been introduced to two ancient food traditions: processing acorns into flour as the Miwok people did in Sonoma Valley for generations, and reducing ripe wine grape juice into the dark, intensely flavored grape molasses called saba. Fiorella shared her knowledge of making fruit vinegars from quince and citrus, and Mike taught me the classic method of turning tomatoes into a highly concentrated *conserva*. I learned from both of them the fundamentals of fermentation. Together, we continue to explore and expand the boundaries of what is possible in the kitchen larder.

A note on how our book is organized: The eight chapters follow the seasons and the order in which Colby brings the harvest into the kitchen at Edge. Within each chapter, our first recipes are for larder items. Main recipes, which incorporate these items, follow. For example, the chapter on herbs features six larder recipes and an equal number of main recipes, including one cocktail. The main recipes don't necessarily depend on your making a larder recipe, and in many cases we suggest commercially prepared ingredients as alternatives. We think you'll agree, however, that once a few of the larder items take up residence in your pantry or refrigerator, they will undoubtedly find their way into your cooking. —*John*

LACTO-FERMENTATION

Wine is among the oldest of fermented products, and working in a dining room owned by a winery is itself an inspiration to create fermented foods. Alcohol is possibly the best-known product of fermentation, and nearly every culture has discovered the natural process of converting the sugar in fruits and grains into alcoholic beverages. Likewise, most cultures practice some form of lacto-fermentation, which is responsible for such favorites as yogurt, sauerkraut, and kimchi.

Ancient cultures relied on fermentation primarily as a method of preserving food. A secondary benefit is that it improves the digestibility of foods, by breaking down proteins and carbohydrates. As chefs, we also love the sharp and intense flavors these foods provide, which enhance and enliven our cooking.

Certain yeasts are used to convert the sugars in grape juice into wine—creating the heady aroma any visitor to a winery notices—but different bacteria, known as *lactobacillus*, are responsible for lacto-fermentation. They are present on the surface of all plants and have the ability to convert sugars into lactic acid, a natural preservative that inhibits the growth of harmful bacteria, thereby preserving food for an extended period. Lactic acid also increases vitamin and enzyme content, making nutrients easier for the body to absorb. Plus, ferments have been shown to actually create nutrients, produce antioxidants, and protect against many harmful pathogens and toxins.

The first time I saw Colby bringing the week's harvest into our kitchen at Edge, I was impressed by the abundance of produce coming from Stone Edge Farm. But when he delivers a huge box of sunchokes or two dozen fist-size kohlrabies, something has to be done other than letting them languish in a forgotten corner of the walk-in refrigerator.

Before Mike and I began working at Stone Edge Farm, we had been cooking together for a few years and already shared a passion for ferments. That made it easy to come up with ideas for a live larder. Together with John, we started a fermentation program and began preserving everything we could. The layers of flavor and depth that ferments bring to our food, along with the health benefits that are so important to us, make these larder items precious to our cuisine. —*Fiorella*

PICKLED RADISHES

Pickling vegetables in vinegar is a creative way to preserve an abundant harvest or be proactive when you have bought too much produce. It is an easy technique that will help you expand your larder. Besides radishes, this recipe works for other root vegetables, such as carrots and turnips, and equally well for cauliflower and peppers, both the sweet and the spicy varieties, such as Limo or Thai chiles. A pickled ingredient gives some dishes the acidity they need and accentuates the flavors of others. Try experimenting with different spices, such as allspice, ginger, bay leaf, or cinnamon, to add a particular note that you like. —Fiorella

1 lb/500 g radishes

3 black or green cardamom pods

1 teaspoon black peppercorns

1 cup/250 ml champagne vinegar

1 cup/250 ml water

2 teaspoons artisanal sea salt

2 teaspoons firmly packed organic light or dark brown sugar

2 cloves garlic

EQUIPMENT

1-pt/500-ml glass jar with lid

Wash the jar and lid in hot, soapy water. Immerse the jar in gently boiling water for 2 minutes. Just before filling, remove the jar from the hot water and shake off any excess. Have the lid ready.

Cut the radishes into ³/₄-inch/2-cm pieces. If they are small, leave them whole.

In a small cast-iron frying pan over low heat, dry-toast the cardamom and peppercorns, shaking the pan occasionally, until fragrant, 2–3 minutes. Set aside.

In a nonreactive saucepan over medium heat, bring the vinegar, water, salt, and sugar to a boil and cook until the sugar and salt dissolve. Add the garlic and toasted spices, reduce the heat, and simmer for 3 minutes. Remove from the heat.

Pack the radishes into the jar and pour the hot pickling liquid over them, leaving ¹/₂-inch/12-mm headspace. Let cool at room temperature on a rack or a kitchen towel, then cap with the lid and refrigerate for at least 2 days before using, to allow the radishes to cure. They will keep for one month in the refrigerator.

LACTO-FERMENTED VEGETABLES

This recipe is ideal for root or other hearty vegetables. The process of fermenting foods is by definition anaerobic, or oxygen-free. By not allowing oxygen to get to the vegetables as they ferment, which is accomplished by submerging them in brine, undesirable yeasts and molds are prevented from growing. You will need a glass jar or crock, a plate that fits just inside the vessel's rim, and a weight to set on the plate to keep the vegetables fully immersed in the liquid. If you use a jar with a lid, make sure to open the jar every other day to allow carbon dioxide to escape. A fermentation airlock, a device that attaches to, or is built into, a jar lid and allows carbon dioxide to escape without permitting new air to enter, can be purchased online and might give you extra confidence that no gas is building up. But an airlock is not essential, and I rarely use one. —Fiorella

---

1 lb/500 g sunchokes or other hearty vegetable

2 cloves garlic

1 bay leaf

5 black peppercorns

1 fresh or dried Thai or other chile of choice

2 cups/500 ml water

2 tablespoons kosher salt

EQUIPMENT

1½ pt/750-ml widemouthed glass jar with lid

Airlock (optional)

Wash the jar and lid in hot, soapy water. Rinse, then immerse the jar in gently boiling water for 10 minutes. Remove the jar from the hot water and shake off any excess. Have the lid ready.

Peel the sunchokes and cut them into halves if big or leave them whole if small. If you are using other vegetables, such as carrots or beets, peel them and cut them into halves or quarters, as needed to fit into the jar. Pack the sunchokes into the jar and add the garlic, bay leaf, peppercorns, and chile. Measure the water in a measuring pitcher, add the salt, and stir with a wooden spoon to dissolve the salt. (We typically use a 2 percent brine for lacto-fermenting vegetables, which is more or less equivalent to 1 tablespoon kosher salt for each 1 cup/250 ml water.) Pour the brine over the sunchokes, then slip a small plate or other thin, flat object into the jar and top it with a weight to keep the sunchokes fully submerged in the brine.

Seal the jar with the lid, with or without an airlock. Keep the jar in a dark place at around 65°F/18°C. The suggested temperature range for ferments is 60°F–68°F/15°C–20°C. If you live in a warm-weather area, check your ferments frequently because the process will be much faster in hotter climates. If you are not using an airlock, every other day remove the lid to release any built-up gases and then recap the jar.

The fermentation process will take about 2–3 weeks. The sunchokes are ready when they have developed a pleasant sour taste. Store them in their brine in an airtight container in the refrigerator for up to 8 months.

CITRUS

WINTER BRINGS THE FRAGRANT AROMA OF A WIDE RANGE OF CITRUS, including several types of lemons, mandarins, and one very prolific kaffir lime whose leaves add a distinct floral note to foods. These colorful winter fruits brighten the sleeping garden while most other trees and plants are taking a break.

Our workhorse in the kitchen is the venerable Meyer lemon, a variety that flourishes here in our California climate and is truly a backyard fruit. It is less pungent than other lemon varieties and, due to its thin skin, less widely distributed. The skin is also smoother, juicier, and sweeter than a regular lemon's. We sometimes chop up whole Meyer lemons, skin and all, and make a wonderful relish with our Stone Edge Farm olive oil, shallots, parsley, and a little salt and pepper.

RECIPES

There are times, though, when the pungent acidity of a Eureka lemon is needed, so we have a few of those. Another tree in our orchard produces beautiful pink variegated lemons with a slightly sweeter and more floral flesh.

The Moroccan technique of preserving lemons in salt and aromatic spices yields a spectacular ingredient that has become a must in our larder. Preserved lemons are essential when we want a bright and salty accent to a dish.

Citrus fruit of all kinds belongs on any chef's short list of necessary ingredients, but lemon is indispensable. Sometimes a squeeze of lemon at the last minute is all a dish needs to really sing. Less formidable in their level of acidity and generally sweeter than lemons are the mandarins and various oranges, notably blood oranges, that frequently find their way

into our desserts and salads. Occasionally we use them in a citrus risotto or a *gastrique* for roasted duck. Both dishes allow citrus to reveal its different character when cooked.

Dry white wines with herbaceous and citrus notes pair well with the acidity in lemon, orange, and grapefruit, including their oily zest. The 20 percent Sémillon in our Stone Edge Farm Sauvignon Blanc lends subtle floral and candied lemon peel hints to the aroma and taste of dishes with citrus as an ingredient.

A word about the covering of a citrus: It is referred to as skin, peel, rind, and zest. It seems that chefs are often more interested in the covering of the fruit, and for good reason. The peel contains a pungent oil that brims with flavor compounds. For adding flavor to sauces or stews, drop in a wide swath of zest, removed with a sharp vegetable peeler. The white part of the peel is usually bitter, so stick to the outer skin, which has all the flavor. For uncooked sauces, relishes, and dressings, we use a Microplane grater to create a very fine zest. —*John*

CITRUS IN THE GARDEN

Untold generations of citrus, from pomelos to mandarins, have been fraternizing in the wilds of East and South Asia. Today, we reap the rewards of their exuberant crossbreeding in the form of an increasingly diverse cornucopia of available citrus. A plant breeder would tell you it's safe to bet that the future holds even more interesting varieties to incorporate into our gardens, farms, and, ultimately, kitchens.

You should probably choose a variety or two to grow in a pot, strategically placed not too far from where you cook. While heavy frost is your enemy, many citrus varieties can survive in a protected area (or dragged into a garage), even in snowy climes. Whether in the ground or a large pot, citrus responds well to a regular application of organic citrus food—three to four times a year, ideally, starting at the last frost of spring and going until two months before the first frost of fall or winter.

Here in Northern California, we generally think of citrus as a winter crop, but thoughtful variety selection can keep your lips puckered for the better part of any given year. December satsumas and Meyers can give way to Murcott mandarins and the pink-fleshed Cara Cara navel oranges in spring. Valencia oranges and Eureka lemons carry us through summer, before the ripening Oro Blanco and Rio Red grapefruits signal the return to peak citrus season as we make our way toward the end of the year.

If you are a true citrus lover and backyard orchardist, you can do your fellow growers a favor by keeping a close eye out for signs of disease. In 2017, California surpassed Florida in citrus production, not because we're growing more but because an infectious disease called citrus greening, or HLB, has been ravaging Florida's citrus crop, along with hurricane damage. The Asian citrus psyllid is an insect pest that transmits the disease, which causes leaves to turn yellow and fruit to ripen unevenly and taste metallic. California's Department of Food and Agriculture is closely monitoring the situation. If you have taken care of your trees' fertility and you still see symptoms, you should remove any infected tree.

To plant your own citrus, a good starting place would be to pick up a dwarf Meyer lemon at your local nursery, where you can learn what citrus varieties can be sourced in your area. If you are new to planting citrus, my book, *Fruit Trees in Small Spaces*, can help. It is widely available, including on Google Books. —*Colby*

PRESERVED LEMONS

Years ago I asked a Moroccan cook I knew to teach me her favorite culinary technique. It didn't involve cooking per se, but she taught me how to make preserved lemons. They have become a favorite ingredient of mine and a perfect use for Meyer lemons. We use these staples of North African cuisine in salads, salsas, and relishes, and, of course, in tagines and stews. It is easy to preserve lemons, and they will last for a year if kept refrigerated. I prefer using Meyer lemons, but any variety will do. —John

---

1 teaspoon pink peppercorns

½ teaspoon black peppercorns

2 cinnamon sticks, broken into small pieces

2 teaspoons coriander seeds

2 dried árbol chiles

7 Meyer lemons, 1½–2 lb/750–900 g

½ lb/250 g artisanal sea salt (about 1½ cups)

About 2 cups/500 ml fresh Meyer lemon juice (from 8–12 lemons)

EQUIPMENT

Mortar and pestle

One 2-qt/2-l glass jar with lid

Wash the jar and lid in hot, soapy water. Rinse, then immerse the jar in gently boiling water for 10 minutes. Remove the jar from the hot water and shake off any excess. Have the lid ready.

In a mortar, combine the pink and black peppercorns, cinnamon, coriander, and chiles and crush lightly with a pestle to release their aromas.

Using a sharp knife and starting at the stem end, cut each lemon into quarters, stopping just short of the blossom end so the base remains intact. Then, one at a time, open each lemon like a flower and sprinkle the interior generously with the salt. Do this in a bowl to make sure none of the salt is lost. As the lemons are salted, pack them into the jar, pushing down on them firmly so they start to release their juices, layering the crushed spices as you go, and using all of the salt. When all the lemons are in the jar, let them sit for 30 minutes to release their juices.

Add lemon juice as needed to cover the lemons, then cover the surface with plastic wrap and top with a weight such as a rock or similar item to keep the lemons immersed. Seal the jar with its lid and store at room temperature for about 1 month. Once a week, give the jar a good shake, remove the lid to release any pressure, and then recap. The lemons are ready when the peels are tender to the bite with fermented tang. At that point, store the lemons in the refrigerator for up to a year.

To use the lemons, remove what you need from the jar. Remove and discard the pulp, briefly rinse away the salt from the peel, and then cut the peel as directed in individual recipes.

Candied Citrus Peel

Here is a great way to preserve your citrus harvest while capturing the fruits' fragrant essential oils. These candies by themselves make incredible treats; if dipped in melted bittersweet chocolate, they are sublime. We use them finely chopped as a bright garnish for ice cream sundaes or folded into a favorite cookie dough, such as gingersnap or chocolate chip. This formula works great for lemons, oranges, and similar citrus whose peels are relatively mild in flavor and not too dense. The peels of more assertively flavored fruits, such as grapefruit or pomelo, should be blanched, before candying, three or four times and the water changed with each blanch or they will be unpleasantly bitter. Look for really fresh organic citrus that hasn't been treated with wax. —Mike

4 lb/2 kg citrus fruits

8 cups/1.6 kg organic sugar, divided

4 cups/1 l water

½ teaspoon cream of tartar

Equipment

Large, heavy enameled-cast-iron, stainless-steel, or other nonreactive pot

Candy (deep-frying) thermometer

Wash the fruits well, then halve and juice them. (Reserve the juice for another use, such as the Preserved Lemons on page 37.) In the pot, combine the juiced citrus halves with water to cover generously and bring to a boil over high heat. If you are candying lemon or orange peels, reduce the heat to a simmer and cook until tender when pierced with a knife tip, 20 minutes or longer, depending on the thickness of the peel. If you are candying grapefruit, pomelo, or other more naturally bitter peels, once the water comes to a rolling boil, blanch for 1 minute, then drain the peels and return them to the pot. Repeat two or three more times to lessen the bitterness. Cover the peels with water once again, bring to a boil, reduce the heat to a simmer, and cook until tender.

Drain well, let the peels cool until they can be handled, and then scoop out and discard the white membrane from the inside of each fruit half. If you are candying grapefruit or pomelo peels, scrape away most of the white pith as you remove the membrane. Cut each citrus half into narrow strips or other shapes.

Rinse the pot thoroughly, then add 6 cups/1.2 kg of the sugar, the water, and the cream of tartar to it and place over medium heat. Bring to a simmer, stirring with a wooden spoon to dissolve the sugar as it heats. Stir the peels into the sugar syrup and return the mixture to a gentle simmer. Clip the candy thermometer onto the side of the pot and simmer the peels gently until they are translucent and the thermometer reads about 225°F/110°C, about 1 hour.

Remove from the heat and drain the peels thoroughly into a colander placed over a heatproof bowl. Discard the syrup.

Line 1 or 2 large sheet pans with parchment paper. In a bowl, toss the peels with the remaining 2 cups/400 g sugar, then spread the peels in a single layer on the pan(s). Let the peels dry at room temperature for 1 day. To store, shake off any excess sugar, transfer to one or more glass jars, cap tightly, and store in a cool, dark place for up to 1 year.

Asparagus Tempura with Meyer Lemon Aïoli   SERVES 4 AS A FIRST COURSE

The secret of a crispy tempura is to keep the batter ice-cold. This batter will also work nicely for other vegetables, such as green beans, zucchini, or artichokes, as well as for squid or fish. It's a good idea to have everything prepped before heating the oil, because once you begin deep-frying, things go quickly. —John

MEYER LEMON AÏOLI

3 cloves garlic

½ teaspoon artisanal sea salt

2 large egg yolks

1 tablespoon fresh lemon juice

1 teaspoon Dijon mustard

⅓ cup/80 ml extra-virgin olive oil

⅓ cup/80 ml expeller-pressed grapeseed
   or other neutral vegetable oil

Finely grated zest of ½ Meyer lemon

TEMPURA BATTER

¾ cup/90 g all-purpose flour

¼ cup/40 g rice flour

1 teaspoon artisanal sea salt

½ teaspoon freshly ground
   black pepper

½ teaspoon fennel pollen (page 68)
   or ground fennel seeds

½ teaspoon ground piment d'Espelette
   or mild chile powder

½ teaspoon ground cumin

1 cup/250 ml plus 2 tablespoons sparkling
   water or club soda

16 asparagus spears

Peanut oil for deep-frying

Finely grated zest of ½ Meyer lemon

Artisanal sea salt

EQUIPMENT

Deep-frying thermometer

To make the aïoli, on a cutting board, mince the garlic with a chef's knife. Then, using the flat side of the blade, mash the garlic with the salt to a paste. In a bowl, whisk together the garlic-salt paste, egg yolks, lemon juice, and mustard until blended. In a small pitcher, combine the olive oil and grapeseed oil. While whisking continuously, start dribbling the oils into the yolk mixture, whisking until it begins to thicken and emulsify. At this point, you can start adding the oils a little more quickly, continuing to whisk until they have been incorporated. If the aïoli seems too thick, whisk in 1 teaspoon water, a few drops at a time. Stir in the lemon zest. Cover and refrigerate until serving.

To make the tempura batter, fill a large bowl with ice and water. In a medium stainless-steel bowl, stir together the all-purpose and rice flours, salt, pepper, fennel pollen, *piment d'Espelette*, and cumin until well mixed. Pour in the sparkling water and whisk just until combined. Do not overmix; a few lumps are fine. Nest the bowl with the batter in the ice water bath and let rest for 30 minutes.

Make a diagonal cut about 1½ inches/4 cm from the stem end of each asparagus and discard the tough end. Make a second diagonal cut at the midpoint of each spear, cutting the spear in half. Fill a large, heavy pot half full with peanut oil and heat over medium-high to 350°F/180°C on a deep-frying thermometer. Line a large sheet pan with paper towels or top with a wire rack and set near the stove.

When the oil is ready, put the asparagus in a large stainless-steel bowl. Add the lemon zest and a sprinkling of salt and toss to coat evenly. Pour the batter over the asparagus. Using tongs or chopsticks, lift several asparagus pieces out of the bowl, letting the excess batter drip off, and plunge them into the hot oil. Deep-fry the pieces, gently circulating them as they cook, until golden brown, 3–4 minutes. Transfer the pieces to the sheet pan and repeat with the remaining asparagus.

Serve the asparagus on a large platter with the aïoli in a bowl, or divide the asparagus and aïoli among individual plates.

Duck Foie Gras Canapés with Citrus Marmalade

I recommend buying prepared duck foie gras au torchon *rather than going to the trouble of making it from scratch. Prepared foie gras is available online from D'Artagnan (www.dartagnan.com) or Hudson Valley Foie Gras (www.hudsonvalleyfoiegras.com) and from high-end specialty grocers such as Dean & DeLuca and The Fatted Calf. If you want to make a foie gras torchon yourself, check out the recipe in the* French Laundry Cookbook, *which works quite well. A word of warning, though: making one is a challenging task for even the professional cook. We make our own at Edge, and when black truffles are in season, we can't resist adding them for the ultimate foie gras. —John*

---

4 thin slices brioche sandwich bread

¼ lb/125 g foie gras au torchon

Artisanal sea salt

2 tablespoons Meyer Lemon Marmalade (page 40) or other lemon marmalade

12 fresh cilantro leaves or small sprigs

Preheat the oven to 400°F/200°C. Using a biscuit cutter 1½ inches/4 cm in diameter, remove 3 rounds from each brioche slice, for a total of 12 rounds. (The remnants from each brioche slice can be dried and processed for bread crumbs.)

Arrange the brioche rounds in a single layer on a sheet pan and bake until crispy and slightly browned, about 5 minutes. Let cool completely before continuing.

Cut the foie gras into 12 uniform slices, each about ¼ inch/6 mm thick. Lay a foie gras slice on top of each brioche toast, then sprinkle with a little salt and top with ½ teaspoon of the marmalade. Garnish each canapé with a cilantro leaf and serve on a platter or board.

Moroccan Orange Salad

The inspiration for this salad comes from Morocco, a land of citrus and spice. In this simple recipe, we flavor orange slices with orange juice, fragrant orange blossom water, cinnamon, and mint. —John

6 navel, Cara Cara, and blood oranges (a mixture)

2 teaspoons Grand Marnier or Cointreau (optional)

½ teaspoon orange blossom water, or 1 teaspoon if not using liqueur

4 dates, pitted and slivered

3 tablespoons sliced almonds, toasted

Ground cinnamon for sprinkling

6 fresh mint leaves, preferably spearmint, torn into small pieces

Juice 1 orange. In a small bowl, stir together the orange juice, liqueur (if using), and orange blossom water.

Using a sharp paring knife, cut ½ inch/12 mm off the top and bottom of each of the remaining 5 oranges to expose the flesh. Stand an orange upright and cut downward, following the contour of the fruit and slicing off the peel and all the pith in wide strips. Cut the orange crosswise into slices ¼ inch/6 mm thick. Repeat with the remaining oranges. Arrange the slices on a serving platter, drizzle them with the flavored juice, and set aside to macerate for 10 minutes.

Arrange the dates and almonds over the orange slices, then top with a generous sprinkling of cinnamon, garnish with the mint, and serve.

Seared Scallops with Meyer Lemon Tiger's Milk, Grapefruit, and Fermented Sunchokes

Piquant tiger's milk, or leche de tigre, is the classic component of a Peruvian ceviche. For the original Incan recipe, tumbo fruit, a close relative of passion fruit, provided the acidity to "cook" the seafood. Later, the Spaniards arrived and introduced lemons, which then became the main sour ingredient. There are many variations of ceviche. In this one, the sweetness of seared scallops balances the acidity of the tiger's milk. —Fiorella

---

Meyer Lemon Tiger's Milk

4 medium-size Meyer lemons

1 medium-size Oro Blanco or other grapefruit

1 clove garlic

1 small red onion, chopped

$1/2$ jalapeño chile, seeded

1 teaspoon peeled and finely grated fresh ginger

$1/4$ cup/60 ml fish stock, or 2 ice cubes

Artisanal sea salt

Seared Scallops

6 large day boat sea scallops

Artisanal sea salt

1 tablespoon clarified butter or ghee

1 tablespoon whole unsalted butter

2 fermented sunchokes, thinly sliced (see Lacto-Fermented Vegetables, page 23)

1 pickled Limo or Thai chile, very thinly sliced (see headnote, Pickled Radishes, page 22)

12 fresh cilantro leaves

To make the tiger's milk, cut off the top and bottom $1/2$ inch/12 mm of each lemon. Stand each lemon on its cut bottom and slice downward between the flesh and the peel, following the contour of the fruit and making sure to remove all the white pith.

Holding a lemon over a small bowl, slice along both sides of each lemon segment, releasing it from the membrane and capturing the segments and the juice in the bowl. Repeat with the remaining lemons. Peel and reserve the grapefruit segments and juice the same way, using a second bowl. Cut the grapefruit segments in half crosswise and set aside for serving.

In a blender, combine the lemon segments, the grapefruit and lemon juices, garlic, onion, jalapeño, ginger, and stock and process until smooth. Strain through a fine-mesh sieve into a bowl. Season with salt, cover, and refrigerate until ready to use.

To sear the scallops, first dry them with a paper towel and season with salt. Heat a 10-inch/25-cm sauté pan over medium-high. When the pan is hot, add the clarified butter, swirl the pan, and then spread the scallops evenly across the bottom. Reduce the heat to medium and let the scallops cook undisturbed for 5 minutes on just one side. Turn the heat to low and add the whole butter, spooning it over the scallops as it melts and browns for 2 minutes longer. Remove from the heat and let rest in a warm spot for a few minutes.

To assemble, divide the tiger's milk among 4 medium-size bowls. Top each serving with $1 1/2$ scallops, the grapefruit segments, 3 or 4 fermented sunchoke slices, 2 or 3 chile slices, and 3 cilantro leaves.

Citrus Risotto

Lemons and blood oranges boldly flavor this lively risotto. Try it for a main dish or with grilled salmon or slices of duck breast. Total cooking time will be about 20 minutes, depending on the rice. If, after absorbing all the stock, the rice is not soft enough for you, just add a little more stock and keep cooking—although in Italy, risotto is always served on the firm side. —John

2 Meyer lemons

2 blood oranges

5½ cups/1.35 l rich chicken or
   vegetable stock

1 tablespoon extra-virgin olive oil

3 tablespoons unsalted butter, divided

1 yellow onion, finely chopped
   (about ¾ cup/115 g)

1½ cups/300 g Arborio or
   Carnaroli rice

⅔ cup/160 ml dry white wine

1 bay leaf

Artisanal sea salt and freshly ground
   black pepper

⅔ cup/85 g freshly grated
   Parmigiano-Reggiano cheese

Using a sharp vegetable peeler, remove all the zest in wide, thin ribbons from 1 lemon and 1 orange, being careful to avoid the white pith. Bring a small saucepan of water to a boil over high heat, drop the zest strips into the water, and boil for 5 minutes. Drain well and let cool, then arrange flat and cut crosswise into tiny julienne. Set aside.

Using a sharp paring knife, cut ½ inch/12 mm off the top and bottom of both lemons and both oranges. Stand a lemon upright and, following the contour of the fruit, cut downward, slicing off the peel and all the pith in wide strips. Then holding the lemon over a small bowl, cut along each side of the membrane between the segments, letting each segment and any juice drop into the bowl. Discard any seeds. Repeat with the second lemon and both oranges.

In a saucepan over medium-low heat, bring the stock to a low simmer. In a large saucepan over medium heat, warm the olive oil and 1 tablespoon of the butter. Add the onion, reduce the heat to medium-low, and cook, stirring frequently with a wooden spoon, until translucent, about 5 minutes. Stir in the rice and cook, stirring often, until well coated and toasted, about 2 minutes. Add the wine and bay leaf and cook, stirring, until the wine is absorbed, about 1 minute or so. Add a ladleful of the stock and continue cooking and stirring until the liquid is absorbed. Add another ladleful and cook, stirring, until it is absorbed. Continue in this manner until the risotto has cooked for about 10 minutes, then add a generous sprinkling of salt, half of the lemon and orange zest, and half of the lemon and orange segments. Continue adding the stock a ladleful at a time and cooking and stirring until absorbed until about ½ ladleful stock remains. This should take about 20 minutes.

Remove the pan from the heat. Add the remaining stock, the remaining 2 tablespoons butter, and most of the cheese and stir to mix. Season with salt and pepper and stir in the remaining citrus zest and segments. Let stand for a few minutes, then spoon into individual shallow bowls, top evenly with the remaining cheese, and serve.

Roasted Duck with Honeynut Squash Purée, Root Vegetables, and Tangerine-Vermouth Gastrique

While traveling in northern Peru, I came across a spectacular variation on the culinary classic of duck flavored with orange. It was combined, according to regional tradition, with squash. Inspired by this dish, I used tangerines from a prolific tree at Stone Edge Farm and quince vinegar, a favorite from our larder, to create the gastrique, a thick sauce that combines vinegar with sugar and typically some sort of fruit. I like Honeynut squash, a petite variety bred for more sweetness and flavor, but a small butternut squash can be substituted. —Fiorella

---

1 whole duck, about 5 lb/2.5kg

2½ teaspoons artisanal sea salt

½ teaspoon freshly ground black pepper

½ teaspoon ground cinnamon

½ teaspoon ground nutmeg

Aromatic herbs: ½ bunch fresh thyme, 10 fresh flat-leaf parsley sprigs, and 2 bay leaves

2 tangerines, halved crosswise

2 Honeynut squashes, or 1 small butternut squash

¼ cup/60 ml chicken stock

Gastrique

2 tablespoons firmly packed organic light brown sugar

1½ cups/375 ml high-quality sweet vermouth

Juice of 5 tangerines (about ¾ cup/180 ml)

½ cup/125 ml Quince Vinegar (page 174) or other fruit vinegar

1 cinnamon stick

3 black cardamom pods

Glazed Root Vegetables

2 kohlrabies, stemmed, quartered lengthwise, cored, peeled, and diced

3 large carrots, peeled and diced

½ cup/125 ml chicken or duck stock

1 tablespoon unsalted butter

Artisanal sea salt and freshly ground black pepper

Preheat the oven to 350°F/180°C.

Remove the neck and the excess fat from the duck, then pat it dry, inside and out, with a paper towel. In a small bowl, stir together the salt, pepper, cinnamon, and nutmeg, then season the duck inside and out with the mixture. Slip the herbs and tangerines into the duck cavity. Set a rack in a deep roasting pan, place the duck, breast side up, on the rack, and set aside uncovered.

Set another rack on a sheet pan. Cut off the stem ends of the squashes, then halve lengthwise and scoop out and discard the seeds and strings. Place the squash halves, cut sides down, on the rack. Bake until tender, 25–30 minutes. Remove from the oven. Leave the oven on and lower the temperature to 325°F.

When the squash halves are cool to the touch, scoop out the flesh and transfer to a food processor or blender. Add the stock and purée until smooth. Transfer to a heavy saucepan and set aside until serving.

Position an oven rack in the bottom third of the oven. Place the roasting pan with the duck on the rack and roast for 1½ hours. Raise the oven temperature to 400°F/200°C.

(continued)

Roasted Duck with Honeynut Squash Purée, Root Vegetables, and Tangerine-Vermouth Gastrique (continued)

Continue roasting the duck until the juices run clear when a thigh is pierced, about 30 minutes more. Remove from the oven and let rest for 30 minutes before carving.

While the duck is resting, make the gastrique. In a small, heavy saucepan over low heat, warm the sugar until it caramelizes. Do not stir it. If it begins caramelizing more at the sides of the pan than at the center, use a wooden spatula to scrape it gently toward the middle. Once the sugar has fully melted and has turned a caramel color, deglaze the pan by adding the vermouth, tangerine juice, and vinegar and stir until the caramelized sugar is combined with the liquids and the mixture is uniform. Add the cinnamon and cardamom and continue to cook over low heat, stirring occasionally, until the mixture is reduced to a syrupy consistency, 15–20 minutes. Strain through a fine-mesh sieve and set aside.

To prepare the vegetables, in a sauté pan over medium heat, combine the kohlrabies, carrots, and stock and cook, stirring occasionally, until almost tender, about 5 minutes. Add the butter and stir until it melts and emulsifies with the liquid, coating the vegetables. Season with salt and pepper.

To assemble the dish, heat the squash purée over low heat until warmed through. Carve the duck into breasts and legs. Portion the legs into drumsticks and thighs. Cut each breast into 2 pieces. Spread a heaping tablespoon of the squash purée onto each plate and top with 1 piece of breast, a drumstick or thigh, and the glazed vegetables. Drizzle some of the gastrique over the duck and vegetables and serve.

from what remains and discard the others. With a small spoon, carefully scoop out the juiced flesh and membrane from the cups. Using a sharp paring knife, cut a very thin slice off the bottom of each cup so it will rest flat. Arrange the cups snugly in a baking dish and freeze for at least 2 hours.

Fill a large bowl with ice and water. Pour the 2 tablespoons water into a small saucepan, sprinkle the gelatin on top, and let it bloom, or soften, for a couple of minutes. Then warm the mixture over low heat just until the gelatin granules melt and are no longer grainy. Add the reserved zest, the sugar, and ¼ cup/60 ml of the orange juice and warm gently, stirring occasionally, until the sugar has completely dissolved. Pour the sugar mixture into the remaining orange juice, stir well, and nest the bowl in the ice water bath until well chilled.

Pour the chilled mixture into the ice cream maker and churn until softly frozen. Transfer to a container and store in the freezer until ready to assemble the cups.

To assemble the cups, remove the ice cream from the freezer. If it is frozen hard, let it soften a little. Fill each frozen orange cup half full with the ice cream and return the cups to the freezer until the ice cream is firm, about 30 minutes. Remove the cups from the freezer again and spoon the sherbet onto the ice cream, mounding it to resemble the shape of an orange. Return the filled cups to the freezer for at least 2 hours before serving.

HERBS

SOME WOULD SAY THAT HERBS ARE THE SOUL OF COOKING, AND WE WOULD AGREE. Just try to imagine food and cookery without the aromatic flavoring and fragrance of herbs. In a recipe such as chicken roasted with potatoes and Meyer lemon, only a little rosemary is used compared to the other ingredients, but the herb's intense aroma is the very essence of the dish. In the garden, a whiff of basil in the warm sunshine will inspire even the most inhibited cook.

Even though we sometimes feel as if we throw the ubiquitous bay leaf into every dish, the flavoring it provides is necessary, if subtle. Just as with nutmeg, you don't want to taste it exactly, but its absence would be noticed. We use bay laurel (*Laurus nobilis*) in our kitchen but occasionally cook with our own California bay laurel, though sparingly due to its intensity.

RECIPES

The potency of the many pungent herbs on our farm comes through in the distinctive taste of the honey from our beehives. Honey is a perfect example of a food that expresses terroir. Unlike a wine, however, the terroir of honey is not based on the soil and other conditions, such as climate and topography, but on the flowering herbs and other plants available to foraging bees.

Herbs are roughly divided between the soft ones, including basil, cilantro, chives, chervil, fennel, parsley, and tarragon, and the sturdier plants with more fibrous stems, such as rosemary, thyme, oregano, marjoram, sage, and savory.

When I'm using soft herbs I leave the bunch intact while immersing it in a bowl of water, then give it a shake and pat it dry in a paper towel. I then begin chopping away at the leaves.

The first inch or two of the stems are fine to chop into the mix, but as they get larger I save them for stocks or marinades.

The sturdier herbs are usually at their best cooked. Rosemary needles and sage leaves, for example, can be stripped from their woody stems, fried crispy, seasoned with salt, and used as a garnish. Whole sprigs of thyme, marjoram, or savory can flavor the oil in a pan roast of chicken or vegetables, and the aromatic oils they release will subtly flavor a dish. The same happens when the sprigs are used in a braise or stew.

You can dry and save most herbs for your larder, and they will be far superior to anything bought at the store and a lot less expensive. Drying them is easy. Tie the stem end of a small bouquet of herbs with a 12-inch/30-cm length of twine or raffia. Hang the bouquet, stems up, indoors in a location with good air circulation for a week, or until the herbs are dry, then strip the dry leaves. Store in a tightly sealed container. —*John*

HERBS IN THE GARDEN

Perennial herbs, such as sage, rosemary, thyme, and oregano, can serve a similar purpose in the garden and the kitchen, providing structure and balance to the landscape or to a dish. Used thoughtfully, they don't necessarily jump out as the first thing you notice, but that carpet of oregano or thyme below the apple tree in the corner of your yard lends a structure that would be missed if it were left out. It's the same with that sprig of thyme folded into the mushrooms I'm going to cook for dinner tonight.

Chives and parsley are two of the herbs we take care to have on hand at all times, and we manage them similarly. They are short-lived perennials that like a bit of protection from hot afternoon sun. We keep a close eye on quality, so that before a given planting starts to get too far past its prime—the stems get tough and lose their brightness, in other words—we can get the next succession growing in another spot.

Here are three more herbs that I appreciate equally in the garden and the kitchen:

> **TRICOLOR SAGE** *(Salvia officinalis)*: This cultivar of common culinary sage has all the flavor you could want and then some, from a beautifully variegated plant that needs hardly any care. The purple-pink new growth stands out against the green and eggshell older growth and makes a sexy garnish for a roast chicken.
>
> **ZAATAR OREGANO** *(Origanum syriacum)*: Many people know of the spice blend that goes by the same name. This is different. Zaatar oregano has sturdy, gray-green foliage that is both velvety and rugged, revealing something of its ability to survive for millennia in its Middle Eastern homeland.
>
> **PASSION PINK** OR **DOT WELLS THYME** *(Thymus vulgaris)*: It's hard to pick a favorite thyme. Both of these have green foliage and pink blooms and are excellent culinary herbs. Showier varieties exist, but there's something perfect about an edible green covering that turns pink in summer.

Each week our garden crew—including Alejo, Jose, and Daniel and occasionally also Gabriel, Ladislau, and Adan—and I harvest seven or eight, and sometimes up to fifteen, different types of herbs for use by the chefs. In addition to what is growing in the main garden at Stone Edge Farm, we keep a rotating selection of herbs growing in containers close to the back door of Edge for use by John, Fiorella, and Mike. If you are short on garden space or have none at all, herbs are easy to grow in even a small pot. Although I can't think of an herb that wouldn't do well in a container, mint is a good choice. It would quickly take over a garden bed if planted directly in the soil. —*Colby*

WILD FENNEL POLLEN

Wild fennel grows along most roads leading in and out of Sonoma. I prefer to find plants that are as far away from traffic as possible, for obvious reasons. To harvest your own pollen, you will need pruning shears and a clean, shallow cardboard box for stashing the whole flowering fennel heads. Since bees are also attracted to the scent of flowering fennel, I avoid stripping a plant bare, preferring to harvest a few heads from each plant and share the rest with the bees. Cut the stalk far enough from the head to give you something to grasp when you later shake the pollen loose. After harvesting, I lay all the heads on large sheet pans or trays to air-dry for a few days.

You can instead place the gathered heads in a large paper bag to dry. The advantage of this method is that all the pollen stays in the bag as the heads are drying. I usually let them dry for a week before shaking them to remove the pollen. Next, I rub the heads between my palms to release even more pollen. At this point, it will be mixed with stems and other plant debris. A quick pass through a coarse-mesh sieve will remove most of the unwanted matter, and the rest can be picked out by hand. Store the pollen in a glass spice jar. An extra step is to label the jar with the harvest date and location, simply for the enjoyment of being reminded of them when you reach for fennel pollen on your larder shelf.

Now, what do you do with this pollen from a weed? The traditional and most obvious use is with pork. The spiced Tuscan *porchetta* derives its flavor from a healthy dusting of fennel pollen. A sprinkle on top of fish definitely wakes it up. It also makes an appearance in the aromatic Middle Eastern spice mixture called *dukkah*, which we use to flavor appetizers. —*John*

Wild Fennel Pollen Dukkah

Alongside many country roads in Sonoma Valley, the prized ingredient wild fennel grows like a weed. In springtime I keep my pruning shears and a paper bag in my car, so I can harvest some of the heads to air-dry and cook with back at Edge. We like this mixture sprinkled on avocado hummus or focaccia bites that have been dipped in olive oil. —John

½ cup/75 g toasted and skinned
  hazelnuts, finely chopped

½ cup/75 g sesame seeds, toasted

½ cup/40 g coriander seeds, toasted
  and finely ground

¼ cup/25 g cumin seeds, toasted and
  finely ground

2 tablespoons fennel pollen
  (see page 68)

1 teaspoon artisanal sea salt

½ teaspoon freshly ground
  black pepper

In a small bowl, combine all the ingredients and stir well. Transfer to a glass jar, cap tightly, and store at room temperature for up to 1 month.

CHEF'S NOTE:

Because the hazelnuts and various types of seeds all toast for different amounts of time, toast them separately in a 350°F/180°C oven or toaster oven until lightly browned. Each one takes 10–15 minutes.

HERB BUTTER

Preserving chopped fresh herbs in the freezer is an option, yet not an ideal one. It is impossible to retain the maximum flavor and texture of herbs by freezing them. When we commingle them with butter and freeze them, however, we have captured the essence of the season. The soft herb butter is rolled up into a log in a sheet of parchment and then allowed to firm up in the refrigerator before going into the freezer. Disks of herb butter can then be sliced into a sauce or tossed with pasta. —John

---

1 teaspoon extra-virgin olive oil

1 large shallot, finely minced

1–1 1/2 cups/30–45 g mixed fresh soft herb leaves, such as flat-leaf parsley, chives, chervil, basil, and/or tarragon

1 lb/500 g unsalted butter, at room temperature

Finely grated zest of 1 lemon

1/2 teaspoon artisanal sea salt

1/4 teaspoon freshly ground black pepper

In a small sauté pan over low heat, warm the olive oil. Add the shallot and cook, stirring occasionally, until tender, about 5 minutes. Remove from the heat and let cool.

Decide which herbs are going into your herb butter. My favorites are parsley, chives, chervil, and tarragon, but any soft-leaf herb will do. Using a salad spinner, wash and dry bunches of each herb. You can pluck each leaf from the stem, but it is not necessary, as stems have great flavor, too. Finely chop all the herbs except chives, which must be finely sliced rather than chopped. Don't worry if the pieces are irregular.

Put the butter in a large bowl, add the cooled shallots, herbs, lemon zest, salt, and pepper, and mix well with a rubber spatula. If you prefer, you can blend the butter and seasonings in a food processor, which results in a smoother texture and a more uniform green color.

Lay a 12-by-20-inch/30-by-50-inch sheet of parchment paper, with a long side facing you, on a work surface. Using the spatula, scoop the butter onto the paper, forming a rough log about 16 inches/40 cm from left to right. Bring the parchment edge nearest you over the roll to cover it, then shape it into a uniform log. Now roll up the log in the parchment and twist the ends in opposite directions to tighten the wrapping.

Refrigerate the log until firm, about 1 hour. To store, unwrap the log and cut into disks 3/4 inch/2 cm thick. Stack the disks, alternating them with 2-inch/5-cm squares of parchment paper, and wrap them first in plastic wrap and then in aluminum foil. They will keep in the freezer for up to 3 months.

SAGE-HONEY SYRUP

Spend just a moment in my wild and woolly front-yard garden and it's clear which culinary herb I favor most. I've lost track of exactly how many sage varieties have established themselves over the years. The leaves of some are small and densely clustered, while others are rotund and droopy. My favorite plant, easily ten years old, has pink and lavender blossoms in the spring and beautiful purple leaves whose shade changes throughout the year. Watching honeybees work the blossoms gave me the idea for this syrup. The earthiness of the honey and sage taste wonderful together, with the raw, piney, and citrusy flavors of the sage softening as they steep in the syrup. —Mike

1 cup/250 ml water

½ cup/125 ml honey

½ cup/100 g organic sugar

½ oz/15 g fresh sage leaves (about 25 leaves)

In a small saucepan over medium heat, combine all the ingredients and bring to a simmer, stirring to dissolve the sugar. Remove from the heat and let cool to room temperature.

Pour the cooled syrup through a fine-mesh sieve into an airtight container, pressing against the leaves with the back of a spoon to extract as much flavor as possible. Cover and store in the refrigerator for up to 1 month.

SAGE-HONEY WHISKEY SOUR

MAKES 1 GENEROUS COCKTAIL

After working in the garden all afternoon it's a pleasure to sit, glass in hand, among the aromatic flowering herbs and listen to the pleasant sound of buzzing bees. —Mike

Ice cubes

2 oz/60 ml bourbon whiskey

¾ oz/25 ml fresh Eureka or Lisbon lemon juice

¾ oz/25 ml Sage-Honey Syrup (above)

1 orange zest strip

1 fresh sage leaf

Chill a short tumbler. Fill a cocktail shaker half full with ice cubes. Add the bourbon, lemon juice, and syrup, cover, and shake well. Strain into the chilled glass. Twist the orange zest strip over the glass, drop it in, and add the sage leaf.

Spring Herb and Lettuce Soup

This verdant, garden-inspired soup is delicious either warm or cold. Although Sonoma's gentle climate encourages tender greens and herbs in the garden year-round, it's the fleeting months of spring, when the wet earth starts to warm, that give us the ideal ingredients. We regularly start our events at Edge with some version of this soup, signaling to our guests that the garden is our primary source of inspiration. The recipe adapts really well to a variety of garnishes, such as crisp, buttery croutons, freshly picked Dungeness crab, or a generous dollop of caviar floating atop a small pool of crème fraîche. We often finish the presentation by adding tiny leaves of the same herbs used in the recipe and sometimes with edible petals from borage, calendula, or nasturtium flowers to brighten the flavor. Nettles can be added to the mix of tender greens, but handle with care! —Mike

---

3 large spring onions, or 1 yellow onion

2 large green garlic stalks, or
    2 cloves garlic

1 medium leek

2 tablespoons extra-virgin olive oil

Artisanal sea salt and freshly ground
    black pepper

1 small russet potato, peeled and thinly
    sliced crosswise

4 cups /1 l vegetable stock or water

1/2 lb/250 g mixed tender greens and
    lettuces, such as spinach, arugula,
    Swiss chard, young mustard greens,
    and romaine and other mild lettuces

2 handfuls mixed fresh tender herb leaves,
    such as flat-leaf parsley, cilantro,
    tarragon, basil, chervil, and celery,
    large stems removed

A few gratings of nutmeg

Fresh lemon juice for seasoning

Herb Oil (page 72) or your best
    extra-virgin olive oil for garnish

Edible flowers and tender herb leaves
    for garnish

Trim the tops from the spring alliums (spring onions, green garlic, and leek) at the point where light green gives way to dark. Split all the stalks in half lengthwise, removing the tough outer layers from each as you go. Rinse the stalks thoroughly in cold water, splaying the layers open as you rinse to dislodge any hidden dirt. Thinly slice the cleaned alliums. If using the yellow onion and garlic cloves, peel and slice them and combine with the leeks.

In a large saucepan over medium heat, combine the alliums, olive oil, and a pinch of salt. Cover and cook, stirring often to prevent browning, until tender, 8–10 minutes. Add the potato and stock, bring to a simmer, add another pinch of salt, and cook, uncovered, until the potato slices are very tender, about 10 minutes.

While the soup base is cooking, fill a large bowl half full with ice and nest a medium bowl in the ice. Have ready an immersion blender or stand blender. Having the ice bath and blender ready to go will ensure that you can chill down the soup rapidly, the key to locking in bright color and flavor.

When the potato slices are tender, raise the heat to medium-high and load all the greens and herbs into the pan, stirring as they wilt into the liquid and the liquid returns to a simmer.

If using an immersion blender, remove the pan from the heat, carefully pour the contents into the bowl nested in ice, and process until smooth, then stir until chilled. If using a stand blender, transfer the soup in two batches, topping the lid with a folded kitchen towel and holding it down firmly to prevent scalding yourself as you purée until smooth. As each batch is ready, pour it into the bowl nested in ice, then stir rapidly until chilled. Grate a very small amount of nutmeg into the chilled soup and season to taste with salt, pepper, and a squeeze of lemon juice.

The soup is delicious served chilled, but if you prefer to serve it hot, wait until the last minute, then reheat gently to preserve its brightness. Ladle into bowls, drizzle with the oil, and garnish with the flowers and herb leaves.

Soft-Leaf Herb Salad with Sunflower Oil and Lemon Dressing

This spring salad of tender herb leaves and lettuces enlivens the palate and stimulates the appetite. For the herbs, choose varieties with soft leaves, such as parsley, dill, basil, mint, cilantro, chervil, or tarragon. The cultivated lettuces can be a mixture of mâche, arugula, and butter lettuce, balanced with a few wild greens like purslane and miner's lettuce. Toss the delicate leaves with your fingertips instead of tongs to avoid bruising them, coating each leaf well with dressing. —John

---

4 handfuls mixed small salad greens, such as arugula, mâche, butter lettuce, purslane, and miner's lettuce

4 heaping cups/120 g mixed fresh soft herb leaves, such as flat-leaf parsley, dill, basil, mint, cilantro, chervil, and tarragon

Artisanal sea salt and freshly ground black pepper

Sunflower Oil and Lemon Dressing

½ teaspoon artisanal sea salt

3 tablespoons fresh lemon juice

7 tablespoons/100 ml expeller-pressed sunflower oil

Fill a very large bowl with cold water, gently immerse the salad greens and herb leaves in the water, and let soak for a few minutes. Using a fine-mesh sieve, lift out the leaves and spin dry in a salad spinner. Alternatively, spread the leaves on kitchen towels to dry. Transfer the dried leaves to a large bowl, cover the bowl with a dry kitchen towel, and chill for 1 hour before serving.

To make the dressing, dissolve the salt in the lemon juice in a small bowl, then whisk in the sunflower oil.

To serve, drizzle some the dressing on the greens and use your fingertips to toss gently. Add more of the dressing and toss until every leaf is well coated (you may have more dressing than needed). Sprinkle with salt and pepper and toss gently again. Taste a leaf and decide if more salt and pepper is needed, then adjust if necessary and serve.

CHEF'S NOTE:

The process of fine-tuning the taste and seasoning of a dish is the hallmark of an accomplished cook. It is a learned skill, and if you haven't acquired it yet, don't hesitate to start practicing. Finding a balance of flavors and seasonings is especially important for a salad like this, which has so few ingredients.

HERB PAPPARDELLE

Tender herbs and leafy greens infused into our egg-rich pasta dough bring fresh brightness to these long, ribbon-like noodles. As the seasons change, we use different combinations of herbs and leaves, producing a pasta that never tastes the same twice. The noodles are a great vehicle to carry the flavorful juices of a chicken or lamb braise. —Mike

---

4 large egg yolks

2 oz/60 g mixed leafy greens, such as arugula and spinach

1 oz/30 g mixed fresh soft-leaf herb leaves, such as basil, chives, tarragon, cilantro, anise hyssop, chervil, and tarragon, tough stems removed, plus more for garnish

1½ cups/190 g all-purpose flour

2 tablespoons semolina flour

Kosher salt

2 disks Herb Butter (page 70), or 3 tablespoons unsalted butter, at room temperature

½ cup/60 g freshly grated Parmesan cheese

Freshly ground black pepper

EQUIPMENT

Hand-crank pasta machine or stand mixer with pasta roller attachment

In a blender, combine the egg yolks, greens, and herbs and process until very smooth. Put the flours in the bowl of a stand mixer fitted with the paddle attachment. Add the herb–egg yolk mixture, using a rubber spatula to scrape in every last bit. Run the mixer on low speed until crumbs of dough begin to form, about 30 seconds.

Lightly flour a work surface and turn the crumbly mixture out onto it. Using your hands, begin to squeeze the dough firmly together until it forms a cohesive mass. Dribble very small amounts of water onto the dough if needed to bring it together, being careful not to add so much that you end up with a sticky dough and, ultimately, unpleasantly textured noodles. Once the mass comes together, continue kneading the dough by aggressively squeezing it, folding it in half, and pushing it down and away with the heel of your hand until it is smooth, uniform, and almost shiny, 5–8 minutes. The kneading takes a fair amount of muscle work, but you will be rewarded with noodles that are tender yet resistant to the bite. Wrap the dough in plastic wrap and hammer down hard on it a few times with a rolling pin to flatten it a bit. Let the dough rest at room temperature for at least 1 hour.

To roll out the dough, set up a hand-crank pasta machine on your countertop or attach the pasta roller attachment to your stand mixer and adjust the rollers to the widest setting. Using the rolling pin, slightly flatten the dough again, then feed it through the rollers. Fold the dough in thirds like a business letter and, leading with a narrow end, roll it through the widest setting once again. This step helps create a squared-off sheet of dough. Continue feeding the dough through the rollers, decreasing the setting width each time and stopping at the next-to-last setting. You should have a long, thin pasta sheet.

Cut the sheet crosswise into about 12-inch/30-cm lengths. Generously flour each length, fold each length in half from top to bottom, and then fold in half again. Now cut the folded dough crosswise into noodles ¾ inch/2 cm wide and gently separate them. If not cooking immediately, set aside in the refrigerator on a lightly floured sheet pan, covered with a clean kitchen towel.

Bring a large pot filled with salted water to a boil and toss
in the pasta. Cook, stirring gently, until tender, about
3 minutes. Drain, transfer to a bowl, and toss with the
butter, coating thoroughly. Divide evenly among warmed
bowls and top with the Parmesan and pepper. Garnish with
the herb leaves.

GRILLED NEW YORK STEAK WITH CHIMICHURRI

Chimichurri is an uncooked sauce popular in Latin America—and now worldwide—for grilled meats and vegetables. It originated in Argentina and is an essential component of asado, *a traditional method for roasting whole animals on a spit. The keys to a chimichurri are to use an abundance of fresh herbs and to serve it within a few hours of preparation. It's okay to use the small stems of parsley and cilantro; just remove the large ones. Although not strictly necessary, the charred chive powder adds a sweet note to the sauce. —Fiorella*

6 New York steaks, 6 oz/170 g each

Artisanal sea salt and freshly ground
   black pepper

CHIMICHURRI

1 cup/250 ml extra-virgin olive oil

2 tablespoons sherry vinegar

1 cup/30 g fresh flat-leaf parsley leaves
   and tender stems, finely chopped

1/2 cup/15 g fresh cilantro leaves and
   tender stems, finely chopped

1/4 cup/10 g fresh oregano leaves,
   finely chopped

1 tablespoon finely diced shallot

1 teaspoon seeded, membranes
   removed, and finely diced serrano
   chile (1 small chile)

1 clove garlic, finely grated

1 tablespoon sumac powder

Artisanal sea salt and freshly ground
   black pepper

1 teaspoon Charred Chive Powder
   (page 73)

Generously season the steaks on both sides with salt and pepper and let stand at room temperature for 1 hour.

Build a hot hardwood or charcoal fire for direct-heat grilling, allowing at least 1 hour for the fire to burn down to the correct temperature. It is ready when a coating of white ash has formed over glowing red embers. Be sure to use plenty of fuel to ensure an adequate bed of embers. In a pinch, a gas grill preheated on high for 10 minutes will suffice.

While the fire is reaching temperature, make the sauce. In a bowl, combine the olive oil, vinegar, parsley, cilantro, oregano, shallot, chile, garlic, and sumac and stir well. Season with salt and pepper and let stand for at least 15 minutes before using.

Clean the grill rack well with a wire brush. Arrange the steaks on the hottest area of the rack and grill, turning once, for about 6 minutes on each side for medium-rare. Transfer to a cutting board or platter and let rest for 10 minutes.

To serve, cut the steaks against the grain into medium-thick slices and arrange on a platter. Spoon some of the sauce over the slices and sprinkle with the chive powder. Serve the remaining sauce on the side.

SLOW-COOKED SALMON WITH SPINACH AND HERB SAUCE SERVES 4

Slow cooking of salmon ensures that the fish cooks evenly. Ask for the center pieces, which will be of uniform thickness, ideally about 1½ inches/4 cm. This recipe also works well with Alaskan halibut or sea bass. We like to use our Mixed Herb Salt to season the fish, but it is also delicious with plain fleur de sel. —John

---

2 large leeks, white part only

1 tablespoon extra-virgin olive oil, plus more for brushing

1 lemon, thinly sliced

8 fresh thyme sprigs, plus more for garnish

4 skin-on center-cut salmon fillets, each 5 oz/155 g and about 1½ inches/4 cm thick

2 teaspoons Mixed Herb Salt (page 72) or artisanal sea salt

Freshly ground black pepper

SPINACH AND HERB SAUCE

2 cups/60 g spinach leaves

½ cup/15 g fresh flat-leaf parsley leaves

½ cup/15 g fresh chervil leaves

2 tablespoons extra-virgin olive oil

1 teaspoon fresh lemon juice

½ teaspoon artisanal sea salt

3 tablespoons water

Preheat the oven to 250°F/120°C.

Leeks tend to collect dirt between their layers, so clean them carefully. First, cut the leeks in half lengthwise, then crosswise into slices ½ inch/12 mm thick. Put the slices in a large bowl filled with cool water and swirl them gently. Using a wire skimmer, transfer the leeks to a colander to drain, then spread them on paper towels to remove any excess water.

Heat a 12-inch/30 cm rondeau or other wide, shallow ovenproof pan over low heat. Add the olive oil and then the leeks and cook, stirring frequently, for 5 minutes. Add the lemon slices and thyme and cook, stirring frequently, for 5 minutes longer. Remove from the heat and spread the leek mixture evenly over the bottom of the pan.

Brush both sides of the salmon pieces with olive oil and then season both sides with the herb salt and pepper. Place the salmon, skin side down, on top of the leek mixture. Bake for 20 minutes. Raise the oven temperature to 275°F/135°C and continue to bake for 5–10 minutes longer. Remove from the oven and let the salmon rest in the pan for a few minutes before serving.

While the salmon is cooking, make the sauce. Fill a bowl with ice and water. Bring a saucepan filled with water to a rapid boil, add the spinach, parsley, and chervil, and blanch for 10 seconds. Scoop out the spinach and herbs with a sieve and immediately plunge them into the ice water bath until chilled. Scoop out the greens, squeeze dry, and chop roughly.

In a blender, combine the blanched greens, olive oil, lemon juice, salt, and water and process on high speed for 10 seconds. Pass through a fine-mesh sieve into a small saucepan and gently warm over low heat just before serving.

To serve, spoon a generous dollop of the sauce over each piece of fish and garnish with thyme sprigs.

GARLIC

SARAH SHIMIZU HAS BEEN SAVING SEEDS and growing some dozen varieties of garlic since 2009. She calls herself the Gypsy Farmer. Her nickname fits her well because every year she farms in a different location of Sonoma or Humboldt County. What she grows is a sublime array of both hard-neck and soft-neck garlics—some European, some Asian, all lovingly started from individual cloves. I've learned from Sarah which varieties are better for storing and which should be used today. Our cool, pitch-black wine cellar is the perfect spot for long-term storage of garlic and other roots.

RECIPES

Cooked garlic loses its sharp pungency and becomes sweet and nutty. Taking this a step further, fermenting whole heads of garlic to render them black and caramelized after weeks of curing results in a sweet, fruity ingredient that works well with salads, sauces, and stews. A supply of garlic confit, along with its by-product, garlic oil, never goes to waste in our kitchen. The soft cloves are easily smashed with the blade of a chef's knife; the oil, which will last for up to a week in the refrigerator, coats cubed bread for garlic croutons.

We use a Microplane grater to add garlic cloves to relishes, pestos, and marinades. When the cell membranes of garlic (or onion for that matter) are penetrated with a knife, they release a pungent substance. Smashing the cells can increase the pungency, especially with garlic that has been in storage awhile, and the grater method limits the harshness.

During the spring, when the garlic plants are still green and their bulbs have not yet formed, we harvest some of them for the kitchen but allow most of them to grow to maturity. It is a springtime ritual for us to work with green garlic, which receives star billing on our menus when we pair it with other seasonal vegetables, such as asparagus, fava beans, peas, and carrots. When the short window of opportunity opens at the conclusion of green garlic season and the arrival of the first potatoes, these two favorites appear happily together on the menu.

As the green garlic scapes, or stalks, dry and wither, it is time to harvest them. The bulbs and attached tops are spread over every available outdoor surface to soak up the sun. Alejo Salinas and his garden crew then braid the stalks into long strands that continue to dry on tree limbs and also festoon our fences and kitchen walls. —*John*

BLACK GARLIC

Black garlic doesn't have the pungency of fresh garlic but instead is fruity and caramelly. Its flavor profile comes from the Maillard reaction, a non-enzymatic chemical reaction produced at a low holding temperature after 3 weeks or up to 40 days in a humid environment. We use black garlic to intensify sauces and salad dressings, such as the one for the stone fruit salad on page 105. —Fiorella

12 heads garlic

EQUIPMENT

Rice cooker

CHEF'S NOTE:

The papery skin of the garlic heads will darken slightly, but only by peeling a clove can you be sure the garlic has turned black or deep brown, depending on the variety. Begin checking the garlic after 2 weeks by removing and peeling a clove to see if it has turned the desired color. If not, check again every other day.

Set the rice cooker to the "keep warm" setting. Stand or stack the garlic heads upright in the bottom of the cooker. Cover the cooker and leave it on the "keep warm" setting for 2–3 weeks for a mild flavor or up to 40 days for a smokier flavor. The garlic will turn a deep caramel black.

The garlic heads will keep in an airtight container at room temperature for up to 2 weeks or in the refrigerator for up to 8 months. Peel the cloves before using.

A savory baked custard starts a meal on an elegant note. These Italian custards adapt to a variety of seasonal ingredients, such as artichokes, asparagus, or morel mushrooms. Sformatini can be made an hour ahead, unmolded, and reheated at serving time. —John

SAVORY SWISS CHARD

3 large spring onions

2 teaspoons extra-virgin olive oil

1 large clove garlic, finely chopped

1 cup/60 g firmly packed chopped
   Swiss chard leaves

Artisanal sea salt and freshly ground
   black pepper

1 tablespoon Garlic and Onion Jam
   (page 97) (optional)

BAKED CUSTARDS

3 tablespoons unsalted butter, divided

1/4 cup/30 g all-purpose flour

1 cup/250 ml whole milk

1 cup/250 ml heavy cream or
   half-and-half

1 fresh bay leaf

A few gratings of nutmeg

Artisanal sea salt and freshly ground
   black pepper

1/2 cup/60 g freshly grated
   Parmesan cheese

4 large egg yolks

2 large egg whites

Salad leaves for garnish

To prepare the savory chard mixture, trim off the root end and half of the green tops from each spring onion, then halve lengthwise and thinly slice crosswise. In a sauté pan over low heat, warm the olive oil. Add the onions and garlic and cook slowly, stirring frequently with a wooden spoon. When the vegetables begin to soften, add the chard and continue cooking and stirring until it has softened and significantly reduced in volume, about 10 minutes. Season lightly with salt and pepper and stir in the jam. Transfer to a bowl.

To make the custards, preheat the oven to 350°F/180°C. Butter eight 3–fl oz/90-ml ramekins with 1 tablespoon of the butter.

In a saucepan over low heat, melt the remaining 2 tablespoons butter. Add the flour, whisk until smooth, and cook for a few minutes, stirring constantly. Pour in the milk and cream while whisking constantly to prevent lumps, then add the bay leaf, nutmeg, salt, and pepper. Continue cooking over low heat, whisking constantly as the mixture begins to thicken. Cook for a few minutes longer, continuing to whisk, until thickened to the consistency of pudding. Remove from the heat, remove and discard the bay leaf, and stir in the Parmesan.

Pass the mixture through a fine-mesh sieve held over a bowl, using a rubber spatula to press everything through. Let cool briefly, then quickly whisk in the egg yolks until thoroughly mixed. Fold the custard into the chard mixture.

In a clean bowl, with a clean whisk, beat the egg whites until soft peaks form. Fold the whites into the chard mixture just until no white streaks remain.

Spoon the chard mixture into the ramekins, filling each one almost to the rim. Place the ramekins in a baking pan large enough to hold them without crowding. Pour hot water into the pan to reach halfway up the sides of the ramekins.

Bake the custards until the tops are slightly browned and beginning to crack, about 25 minutes. Remove the pan from the oven, then carefully transfer each ramekin to a work surface or wire rack and let cool for 10 minutes.

To serve, run a paring knife around the inside edge of each ramekin to loosen the custard sides, then invert, with a firm knock, onto a wooden cutting board. Using a small offset spatula, transfer each custard, top side up, to a plate. Garnish each plate with salad leaves.

CHEF'S NOTE:

The custards can be baked up to 2 hours before serving. To reheat, arrange the unmolded custards, top sides up, on a sheet pan lined with parchment paper and warm in a 350°F/180°C oven for 5 minutes.

SALT COD FRITTERS
WITH SKORDALIA

Spanish galleons of long ago were loaded with the salted harvest from the great stocks of Atlantic codfish that sustained sailors on their mission to explore the Americas. Although the need to preserve fish diminished over time, a fondness for the pungent flavor and firm texture of salt cod has endured throughout Mediterranean Europe. Here, the savory salt cod and garlic purée known as brandade, *popular in the south of France, is transformed into a crispy fried treat.* Skordalia, *the creamy, mildly piquant Greek dipping sauce similar to aïoli, is the perfect foil for the fritters. They taste great with a glass of Sauvignon Blanc.* — Mike

SALT COD FRITTERS

1/2 lb/250 g salt cod fillet

2 cloves garlic, unpeeled and smashed, plus 1 clove garlic, peeled

2 thick yellow onion slices

2 fresh thyme sprigs

1 bay leaf

2 cups/500 ml whole milk

1/2 lb/250 g russet potatoes, peeled and thinly sliced

2 tablespoons chopped fresh flat-leaf parsley

1 tablespoon chopped fresh chives

3 tablespoons extra-virgin olive oil

Small pinch of cayenne pepper

Artisanal sea salt and freshly ground black pepper

SKORDALIA

1/2 lb/250 g russet potatoes, peeled and cut into large, uniform pieces

Kosher salt

3 cloves garlic

1/2 cup/125 ml extra-virgin olive oil

Tiny pinch of cayenne pepper

Artisanal sea salt

Fresh lemon juice for seasoning

Tempura Batter (page 42)

Expeller-pressed sunflower, grapeseed, or other neutral vegetable oil for deep-frying

Artisanal sea salt

Lemon wedges for serving

EQUIPMENT

Deep-frying thermometer

Ricer (optional)

To make the fritters, immerse the salt cod in a bowl of cold water and refrigerate for 24 hours, changing the water three times. Drain the cod, transfer to a saucepan, and add the 2 smashed garlic cloves, the onion, thyme, bay leaf, and milk. Bring to an active simmer over medium heat, reduce the heat to low, and poach the salt cod at a gentle simmer until it flakes easily when tested with a knife tip, about 5 minutes.

Using a wire skimmer, transfer the salt cod to a plate. Add the potatoes to the pan, raise the heat to medium, and return the liquid to an active simmer. Cook until very tender when pierced with a knife, about 10 minutes. While they cook, pick through the warm salt cod, removing any bones, cartilage, and skin. When the potatoes are ready, drain well and discard the milk, onion, garlic, and thyme sprigs.

In a bowl, mash the salt cod well with a fork. Pass the potatoes through a medium-mesh sieve or the ricer into the bowl with the cod, then finely grate the remaining garlic clove into the bowl. Add the parsley, chives, olive oil, cayenne, and a couple of grinds of black pepper and thoroughly mix everything together with a wooden spoon. Taste and add salt if needed.

(continued)

To make the skordalia, combine the potatoes with water to cover in a small saucepan, season lightly with kosher salt, and bring to a simmer over medium heat. Cook until tender when pierced with a knife, 10–15 minutes, depending on their size. Scoop out about ¼ cup/60 ml of the potato water and reserve. Drain the potatoes and spoon them onto a plate. Cover the hot potatoes with a clean kitchen towel to capture their steam. This will make them fluffy and give the sauce a nice consistency. Once the potatoes are mostly cooled, transfer them to a food processer and add 1 tablespoon of the reserved potato water. Finely grate the garlic cloves over the potatoes, then blend just until the potatoes and garlic are combined. With the motor running, slowly drizzle in the olive oil through the feed tube, followed by the cayenne, a pinch of sea salt, and a generous squeeze of lemon juice. Adjust the sauce with small dribbles of the potato water until it has the consistency of mayonnaise. Taste and adjust the seasoning with sea salt and lemon juice if needed. You should have about 1 cup/250 ml.

To cook the fritters, make the tempura batter and nest the bowl in an ice water bath as directed in the asparagus tempura recipe.

Fill a large, heavy pot half full with the oil and heat over medium-high to 350°F/180°C on the deep-frying thermometer. Line a large sheet pan with paper towels and set near the stove.

Shape half of the fritter mixture into walnut-size spoon-fuls and carefully submerge them in the batter. Using a fork, lift out the fritters one at a time and drop them gently into the hot oil. Deep-fry, stirring gently so they color evenly, until crisp and golden brown, 3–5 minutes. Using a slotted spoon, transfer the fritters to the sheet pan to drain, then sprinkle lightly with salt. Repeat with the remaining fritter mixture.

Arrange the fritters on a plate and serve warm with the lemon wedges and the skordalia.

Turkish Yogurt and Green Garlic Soup with Mint and Cumin

The yogurt soups of Turkey are deservedly famous. Turkish cooks make phenomenal use of seasonal vegetables, combining them with the brightness and depth of flavor that only yogurt has. In this version we use lots of green garlic cooked long and slow to bring out the tender shoots' sweetness. We finish the soup with a drizzle of browned butter, which helps ground the tang of the yogurt and adds a wonderfully complex flavor. If you don't have the time to make a homemade stock, simply use water. It will still be great. —Mike

---

6 tablespoons/90 g unsalted butter, divided

¼ cup/50 g basmati, Calrose (California-grown medium grain), or other good-quality white rice

Kosher salt

¾ lb/375 g green garlic stalks, dark green tops and tough outer layers removed

2 tablespoons extra-virgin olive oil

½ teaspoon cumin seeds

½ teaspoon Aleppo or other red chile flakes

Artisanal sea salt and freshly ground black pepper

1 large egg

1½ teaspoons all-purpose flour

2 cups/500 ml chicken or vegetable stock

1½ cups/375 g plain Greek yogurt

10 fresh mint leaves, torn

In your smallest pan, over medium heat, melt 4 tablespoons/60 g of the butter and cook, stirring occasionally, until the milk solids separate from the butterfat. Continue cooking until the butter turns a deep golden brown and perfumes the air with the fragrance of toasted nuts, about 2 minutes. The butter can easily burn once it has browned, so immediately pour it into a small bowl and set aside.

Bring a small saucepan filled with lightly salted water to a boil over high heat. Add the rice and cook until tender, about 12 minutes. Drain and reserve.

Split the garlic stalks in half lengthwise and rinse well under cold running water to remove any dirt, then thinly slice crosswise. In a saucepan over medium heat, melt the remaining 2 tablespoons butter with the olive oil and stir in the green garlic. Add the cumin, chile flakes, and a generous pinch of artisanal salt. Cook, stirring frequently, until the green garlic is very tender and tastes sweet, about 20 minutes.

When ready to serve, whisk together the egg and flour in a large bowl until a paste forms. Slowly whisk in a little stock to thin the paste, then stir in the remaining stock and the yogurt. Pour this mixture over the green garlic mixture and warm over medium heat, stirring constantly, to just below a boil. Don't let the soup boil or it will lose its smooth, luscious consistency. Taste and add artisanal salt if needed.

To serve, divide the rice evenly among warmed bowls, then ladle the soup over the top. Garnish each serving with a generous drizzle of browned butter, some mint, and a grind of pepper.

Chicken Cooked under a Brick with Garlic and Herbs

Our version of the Tuscan classic pollo al mattone *uses boneless chicken thighs. The key is the* mattone, *the heavy weight that flattens the chicken, allows it to cook fast and evenly, and helps to crisp the skin. Ask the butcher for large thighs, ideally 7 to 8 ounces/220 to 250 g each. At home I have a small outdoor gas grill that I've outfitted with a griddle. It is perfect for this recipe and for griddling vegetables, fish, and meat. For maximum flavor, however, a wood fire is superior. —John*

---

4 skin-on, bone-in chicken thighs,
  7–8 oz/220–250 g each

Artisanal sea salt and freshly ground
  black pepper

4 cloves garlic

3 green onions, dark green tops and
  outer papery layer removed, halved
  lengthwise, and thinly sliced
  crosswise

1 tablespoon Garlic and Onion Jam
  (page 97) (optional)

1 cup/30 g loosely packed fresh sage,
  oregano, thyme, and flat-leaf parsley
  leaves, in roughly equal amounts

Finely grated zest of 1 lemon

3/4 teaspoon Aleppo or other red chile
  flakes

3 tablespoons extra-virgin olive oil,
  divided

Leafy Green Salad

4 handfuls tender baby greens

1 tablespoon extra-virgin olive oil

2 teaspoons fresh Meyer or other
  lemon juice

Artisanal sea salt and freshly ground
  black pepper

Equipment

Mortar and pestle

A second griddle for weight, or
  2 standard-size bricks wrapped in foil

Liberally season the chicken on both sides with salt and several grinds of pepper and place, skin side up, on a rack in a pan. Refrigerate uncovered for a few hours to air-dry.

Using the mortar and pestle, pound together the garlic, onions, Garlic and Onion Jam, herbs, lemon zest, chile flakes, and a pinch of salt until roughly incorporated, then add 2 tablespoons of the oil and continue to pound until reduced to a paste. Slather the mixture over both sides of the chicken thighs and return them to the refrigerator for 2 hours to marinate.

Build a medium-hot hardwood fire for direct-heat grilling, allowing at least 1 hour for the fire to burn down to a coal and ash bed at least 6 inches/15 cm deep. Ideally, the grill will have an adjustable rack to allow maximum control. Place a griddle large enough to accommodate the chicken in a single layer on the grill rack and heat for 10 minutes. If using a gas grill, heat the grill to medium-hot, then top with the griddle and preheat for 10 minutes.

Oil the griddle with the remaining 1 tablespoon oil and top with the chicken, skin side down, in a single layer. If you have a second griddle the same size, place it on the chicken. If not, top the chicken with the traditional weights: bricks wrapped in aluminum foil, using a single brick for 2 thighs. Cook for 5 minutes, remove the griddle or bricks, flip the chicken over—the skin should be nicely browned—and replace the weight(s). Cook for another 5 minutes and repeat the flipping, so the thighs are once again skin side down. Cook for another 5 minutes and remove the weight(s). The chicken should be opaque throughout when tested with a knife tip.

Just before the chicken is ready, make the salad. In a bowl, toss the greens with the olive oil and lemon juice and season with salt and pepper.

Transfer the chicken to individual plates, arrange the salad alongside, and serve.

PORK AND GARLIC STIR-FRY

Stir-fry originated in China centuries ago. In Peru, our large Chinese community created a fusion of the two countries' ingredients, resulting in a much-loved cuisine. Stir-frying uses a small amount of oil or fat and high heat to preserve the colors and textures of ingredients and to seal in their flavors. —Fiorella

---

1½ lb/750 g boneless pork loin, cut into 1-inch/2.5-cm cubes

1 teaspoon artisanal sea salt

¼ teaspoon freshly ground black pepper

¼ teaspoon ground cumin

⅛ teaspoon ground cinnamon

3 tablespoons expeller-pressed sunflower oil, divided

1 small red onion, finely chopped

2 heads bok choy, sliced crosswise

1 Anaheim chile, julienned

4 cloves garlic, minced

1 tablespoon peeled and grated fresh ginger

1 tablespoon tamari

¼ cup/10 g loosely packed fresh cilantro leaves

¼ cup/10 g loosely packed fresh basil leaves

Steamed jasmine or basmati rice for serving

Season the pork with the salt, pepper, cumin, and cinnamon.

Heat a cast-iron frying pan or a wok over high heat. Add 2 tablespoons of the sunflower oil, and when the oil is hot, add the pork and sauté until golden brown on all sides, about 6 minutes. Transfer to a plate.

Add the remaining 1 tablespoon oil to the pan and then, one ingredient at a time, add the onion, bok choy, chile, garlic, and ginger, sautéing briefly after each addition. When all the ingredients have been added, continue to sauté for 3–4 minutes and then add the tamari. Turn off the heat, return the pork to the pan, add the cilantro and basil, and toss lightly. Taste and adjust the seasoning with salt and pepper if needed.

Serve with the rice.

POTATOES

DON'T GO LOOKING FOR LARDER RECIPES IN THIS CHAPTER. Potatoes, due to their starchy nature, don't provide the ideal cell structure for transformation into something more delicious. Sure, you can slice or shred potatoes and dehydrate them, but unless you are into backpacking or preparing for the Apocalypse, stick to the fresh ones and store them in a dry, cool place to extend their life. So why have a chapter devoted to an ingredient we do not preserve? The answer is simple. We love growing, cooking, and eating potatoes.

The average market may carry only three or four kinds of potatoes, choosing to overlook the more interesting and tasty ones that number in the hundreds. The Andes region actually boasts thousands of distinct varieties, their diversity based on elevation, location, and cultivation practices.

RECIPES

Perhaps because of potatoes' agreeable disposition and ability to soak up flavors around them—making them the perfect foil for the garlic, herbs, spices, and olive oil in our larder—the effect of terroir on potatoes is readily apparent. The weather, soil, elevation, and natural flora and fauna all reveal the identity of a particular place, which can be tasted in a finished potato dish.

When we walk with Colby in the garden, he points out the raised furrowed rows of heirloom potatoes growing in mounded berms that support the plants as they get bigger. At the head of each row is a wooden marker listing German Butterball, Rose Finn Apple, Russian Banana, Austrian Crescent, and at least a dozen other names. The last row, La Ratte, is devoted to the fingerling beloved by chefs in France and, more and more, in the States. This is the variety that French chef Joël Robuchon uses for his signature potato purée. Later in this chapter,

a simple recipe, New Potatoes in Parchment, pays homage to the rich, nutty-tasting La Ratte.

Potatoes are roughly divided into three categories. The first is starchy potatoes, including the russet and most sweet potatoes. These are at their best baked, but they make a decent mash and, of course, outstanding fries. All-purpose potatoes with medium starch, such as Yukon Gold, Norland Red, and Kennebec, can go in multiple directions—mashed or fried or used in gratins and salads. The third group is known by the unfortunate descriptor *waxy*. I prefer *yielding*, which describes how the cooked potato reacts when pierced by a small knife. The list grows longer in this potato group. Rose Finn Apple, Red Thumb, Magic Molly, and La Ratte all fall within this category and are ideal for salads and for roasting and even for mashing, if you don't mind peeling a bunch of little potatoes. —*John*

POTATO RÖSTI

This deceptively simple recipe calls for a certain commitment to learning a technique that requires a bit of mastery. The recipe itself is easy, but turning out a crispy and well-formed rösti, or potato cake, takes a little practice. The traditional method for flipping a rösti is to angle the pan away from you slightly and flick the wrist forward and then immediately backward in a circular motion. As this does take practice, it is also permissible to slip a small metal spatula underneath the cake and simply flip it over in the pan. —John

5–6 large Yukon Gold, Katahdin, or russet potatoes, about 2 lb/1 kg

1 tablespoon plus 1¼ teaspoons artisanal sea salt

4 grinds of black pepper

Clarified butter or expeller-pressed grapeseed, sunflower, or other neutral vegetable oil for the pan

In a 4-qt/4-l saucepan, combine the potatoes, 1 tablespoon of the salt, and water to cover generously and bring to a boil over high heat. Reduce the heat to medium and cook for 10 minutes, then drain. Let the potatoes cool until they can be handled, then peel them, place in a covered container, and refrigerate for 1 hour.

Preheat the oven to 350°F/180°C. Line a large sheet pan with parchment paper.

Using the large holes on a box grater or a food processor fitted with the grater disk, coarsely shred the potatoes and transfer to a large bowl. Add the remaining 1¼ teaspoons salt and the pepper and mix everything gently with a large metal spoon.

Heat an 8½-inch/21.5-cm French-style carbon-steel pan over medium heat. If you lack a proper steel pan, a nonstick pan of similar size will work. Cover the bottom of the pan with a generous sheen of clarified butter, measure 1 cup/185 g grated potatoes, and add to the pan. Using a heat-resistant rubber or flat wooden spatula, press down on the potatoes to form a cake and then herd any shreds around the edge toward the whole to form a perfect disk. Cook on the first side until golden brown, about 5 minutes. Flip the disk (see the headnote for the flipping technique) and cook on the second side until golden brown, about 5 minutes longer. Carefully transfer the potato cake to the sheet pan. Repeat with the remaining potato mixture to make a total of 4 röstis, adding more butter to the pan as need.

When all of the röstis are cooked, reheat them in the oven for a few minutes until hot, then serve.

New Potatoes in Parchment

Diners express a sense of delight and anticipation when these puffed-up parchment paper packages are brought to the table. It's fun to let your guests open their individual packages with a pair of scissors or a sharp knife. When the parchment is cut open and the steam is released, the enticing aroma of potatoes, onions, garlic, and fresh thyme fills the air. The best way to slice the raw potatoes into coins is to use a mandoline, the Japanese "Benriner" being my favorite. —John

---

6–10 green onions, depending on size

3½ tablespoons extra-virgin olive oil, divided

4 cloves garlic, thinly sliced

Artisanal sea salt and freshly ground black pepper

2 tablespoons chopped fresh thyme leaves

6 cups/750 g thinly sliced new fingerling potatoes, such as La Ratte, in slices ⅛ inch/3 mm thick

1 tablespoon unsalted butter, cut into ½-teaspoon pieces

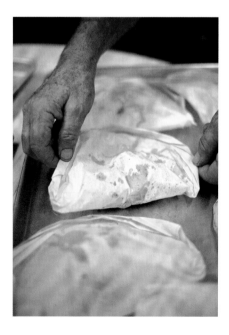

Position a rack in the top third of the oven and preheat the oven to 425°F/220°C. Have ready 2 sheet pans. Cut 6 sheets parchment paper, each 12 by 15 inches/30 by 38 cm.

Cut off half the green tops from each green onion and discard. Cut each onion in half lengthwise, remove the outer papery layer, and then thinly slice crosswise.

Heat a sauté pan over low heat. Add 1½ tablespoons of the olive oil, the green onions, and the garlic and cook slowly, stirring occasionally with a wooden spoon to keep the vegetables cooking evenly, until beginning to soften. Season lightly with salt and pepper, add the thyme, and continue cooking, stirring occasionally, until the onions and garlic are soft but not browned, about 8 minutes total. Remove from the heat and let cool.

While the onion mixture is cooling, fold each parchment sheet in half from left to right and use your thumb to create a sharp crease. Unfold the sheets and arrange them on a work surface with all the creases running vertically. Working 1 inch/2.5 cm to the right of each crease, spread 2 tablespoons of the onion mixture. If you have leftover onion mixture, divide it evenly among the sheets. Place 1 cup/125 g of the sliced potatoes on top of the onion mixture, gently spreading them out ¾ inch/2 cm thick. Season the potatoes with salt and pepper, then drizzle each portion with 1 teaspoon of the remaining olive oil and top with ½ teaspoon of the butter.

Begin by folding the left side over the filling to meet the right edge. Then, starting at the bottom corner, make a 1-inch/2.5-cm sharp fold, pressing with your thumb to create a good crease. Continue to fold and crease, moving counterclockwise around the semicircle, until you reach the end. Your package will have one straight side and one curved side. Seal the last opening securely by pinching it together with your finger and thumb and twisting firmly.

Divide the packages between the sheet pans and bake for 20 minutes. The parchment will puff up and turn pale brown. Serve the packages on individual plates.

Potato and Green Garlic Ravioli

Here you'll find a versatile formula for a silky egg-rich pasta dough. In this recipe we roll and cut the dough into ravioli stuffed with a comforting filling of green garlic and mashed potatoes, but any well-seasoned filling can stand in. Finely chopped mushrooms sautéed with shallot and thyme would be great, as would well-drained top-quality ricotta mixed with a little lemon zest. The salt cod and mashed potatoes we use for our fritter recipe (page 101) would make a delicious filling, too. Thinking beyond filled pasta, you can simply roll and hand-cut this dough into pleasing widths and serve with a pan sauce from pot roast, a simple tomato sauce, or just butter and cheese. An optional garnish of delicate herb leaves, flower blossoms, or microgreens creates another layer of enticement. —Mike

---

PASTA DOUGH

1 1/2 cups/190 g all-purpose flour

7 large egg yolks

1 teaspoon water

RAVIOLI FILLING

1 lb/500 g Yukon Gold or other medium-starch potatoes, peeled and cut into 1-inch/2.5-cm pieces

Big pinches of kosher salt

3 oz/90 g green garlic stalks, dark green tops and tough outer layers removed

2 fresh thyme sprigs

4 tablespoons/60 ml extra-virgin olive oil

Artisanal sea salt and freshly ground black pepper

6 tablespoons/45 g freshly grated Parmesan cheese

Kosher salt

Unsalted butter for serving

Freshly grated Parmesan cheese for serving

EQUIPMENT

Food mill (optional)

Hand-crank pasta machine or stand mixer with pasta roller attachment

Fluted ravioli cutting wheel

Water bottle atomizer

To make the dough, put the flour in a stand mixer fitted with the paddle attachment. In a small bowl, whisk together the egg yolks and water just until blended. With the mixer on low speed, add the yolks to the flour and mix just until crumbs of dough begin to form, about 1 minute.

Lightly flour a work surface and turn the crumbly mixture out onto it. Using your hands, begin to squeeze the dough firmly together until it forms a cohesive mass. Dribble very small amounts of water onto the dough if needed to bring it together, being careful not to add so much that you end up with a sticky dough. Once the mass comes together, continue kneading the dough by aggressively squeezing it, folding it in half, and pushing it down and away with the heel of your hand until it is smooth, uniform, and almost shiny, 5–8 minutes. Wrap the dough in plastic wrap and hammer down hard on it a few times with a rolling pin to flatten it a bit. Let the dough rest at room temperature for at least 1 hour.

While the pasta dough is resting, make the filling. In a saucepan, combine the potatoes, kosher salt, and water to cover generously and bring to a boil over high heat. Reduce the heat to medium and cook until tender when pierced with a knife, 10–15 minutes. Drain well, then return the potatoes to the pan off the heat and cover with a kitchen towel to capture their steam. They will be fluffier when processed.

While the potatoes cook and steam, prepare the green garlic. Split the stalks in half lengthwise and rinse well under cold running water to remove any dirt, then slice crosswise as thinly as possible. In a small saucepan over medium-low heat, combine the green garlic, thyme sprigs, 2 tablespoons of the olive oil, and a pinch of sea salt and cook, stirring occasionally, until the green garlic is tender, about 5 minutes. Once tender, scrape the green garlic and any juices from the pan into a bowl and discard the thyme sprigs.

(continued)

Pass the potatoes through the food mill fitted with the coarse disk or a coarse-mesh sieve into the bowl with the green garlic. Add the remaining 2 tablespoons olive oil, the cheese, and a couple of grinds of pepper and stir everything together without overmixing. Season to taste with sea salt.

To make the ravioli, have ready the ravioli cutting wheel, the water bottle atomizer set on wide spray, and a small bowl of flour. Dust a large sheet pan with flour and have a clean kitchen towel nearby. Set up the hand-crank pasta machine on your countertop or attach the pasta roller attachment to your stand mixer and adjust the rollers to the widest setting. Using the rolling pin, slightly flatten the dough again, then feed it through the rollers. Fold the dough in thirds like a business letter and, leading with a narrow end, roll it through the widest setting once again. Continue feeding the dough through the rollers, decreasing the setting width each time and stopping at the next-to-last setting. You should have a long, thin pasta sheet.

Cut the sheet crosswise into thirds. Lay 1 sheet on the work surface. Cover the other 2 sheets with a big sheet of plastic wrap so they don't dry out. Working quickly to prevent drying, spoon teaspoon-size mounds of the filling in a row down the middle of the sheet, spacing them evenly about 1 inch/2.5 cm apart. Lightly spray the dough with the water atomizer, then fold the sheet in half lengthwise over the filling. With lightly floured fingers, press down on the dough around and between the mounds of filling. Next, with the ravioli cutter, cut along the bottom of the folded dough to make a clean bottom edge and then cut between the mounds to separate them into individual ravioli. Quickly press the dough around each mound again to make sure it is sealed securely, then transfer the ravioli to the sheet pan and cover with the kitchen towel. Continue to assemble more ravioli with the remaining pasta sheets and filling and add them to the sheet pan in a single layer. Store the ravioli in the refrigerator in a covered container until ready to cook or for up to 1 day. They can also be frozen on a sheet pan and then transferred to lock-top plastic bags to freeze for future use.

Bring a large pot of generously salted water to a boil. Slide the ravioli into the boiling water and cook until tender, 3–4 minutes. Using a wire skimmer or large sieve, scoop out the ravioli and transfer to a large serving bowl. Toss with the butter and a splash of pasta cooking water and serve. Pass the cheese at the table.

Potatoes, Shrimp, and Avocado with Chermoula

Peru has some three thousand types of heirloom potatoes and, not surprisingly, multiple ways of cooking and using them. One way that we Peruvians enjoy this ancient and cherished tuber is by making causa. *Originating in pre-Columbian times, this cold dish has evolved from one of just chiles and mashed potatoes to the addition, in the colonial and republican eras, of seafood or chicken. Contemporary* causas— *such as this one incorporating the North African marinade* chermoula—*reflect the changing landscape of culinary tastes and innovation. Fresh Pink Hopper shrimp from Florida are, in my opinion, the tastiest fresh shrimp available, but if you cannot find them, high-quality frozen Gulf shrimp are an acceptable substitute.* —Fiorella

---

Chermoula

1/4 teaspoon cumin seeds

1/4 teaspoon coriander seeds

1 clove garlic

1/2 teaspoon sweet paprika

1/2 teaspoon ground Aleppo chile

4 tablespoons/60 ml extra-virgin olive oil, divided

2 tablespoons fresh lemon juice, divided

1/2 cup/15 g fresh cilantro leaves and stems, chopped

1/2 cup/15 g fresh flat-leaf parsley leaves and stems, chopped

1/4 cup/10 g fresh mint leaves

Finely grated zest of 1 lemon

Artisanal sea salt and freshly ground black pepper

Causa

1 pound/500 g russet or medium-starch potatoes such as Yukon Gold

Kosher salt

2 tablespoons expeller-pressed sunflower oil

2 tablespoons fresh lime juice

1 1/2 teaspoons ancho chile powder

Artisanal sea salt and freshly ground black pepper

1 tablespoon expeller-pressed avocado oil

12 extra-large Pink Hopper or other shrimp, about 1/2 lb/250 g total weight, peeled and deveined

1 avocado, sliced

Equipment

Mortar and pestle

Ricer

To make the chermoula, in a small frying pan over low heat, toast the cumin and coriander seeds, shaking the pan occasionally, until fragrant, 3–4 minutes. Pour into the mortar, let cool, then begin breaking them down with a pestle. Add the garlic, paprika, and Aleppo chile and continue pounding and grinding to make a paste. Add 2 tablespoons of the olive oil and 1 tablespoon of the lemon juice and work them into the paste, then work the cilantro, parsley, and mint into the paste. Finish with the remaining 2 tablespoons olive oil and 1 tablespoon lemon juice and the lemon zest. Season with salt and pepper. The ingredients should look fully incorporated but still chunky and lively. Set aside until ready to serve.

To make the causa, in a saucepan, combine the potatoes, water to cover generously, and enough kosher salt for the water to taste moderately salty. Bring to a boil over high heat, reduce the heat to medium, and cook until the potatoes are tender and easily pierced with a thin knife or cake tester. The timing will depend on their size. Drain in a colander and let cool for 5 minutes, then peel the still-warm potatoes and pass them through the ricer into a bowl.

(continued)

In a small bowl, whisk together the sunflower oil, lime juice, and chile powder and season with sea salt and pepper. Add to the potatoes and mix well. Set aside at room temperature while you cook the shrimp.

To finish the dish, in a frying pan over medium-high heat, warm the avocado oil. Add the shrimp and cook, turning once, until opaque throughout, about 2 minutes on each side. Transfer the shrimp to a warmed plate.

To serve, place a small amount of causa on each plate. Arrange 3 shrimp around it. Drizzle a little chermoula on the shrimp and garnish with the avocado.

CRISPY POTATOES WITH MUSHROOMS, HYSSOP, AND GARLIC CONFIT

SERVES 4

Every year we collaborate with Colby, our garden director, to source different seeds for the farm. The heirloom new potatoes he grows are delightful to work with. Two great choices for pairing with them are cultivated king trumpets, because of their meaty texture, and wild porcini, when available. A large anise hyssop plant, loved by the bees, grows abundantly outside the kitchen and inspired me to combine honey and hyssop. —Fiorella

---

GARLIC-HONEY DRESSING

3 cloves garlic confit (page 93)

3 tablespoons extra-virgin olive oil

¼ cup/60 ml fresh lemon juice

1 tablespoon honey

Artisanal sea salt and freshly ground
    black pepper

6 small to medium king trumpet
    mushrooms

12 small purple potatoes or other variety

Kosher salt

5 black peppercorns

1 árbol chile or similar small fresh
    or dried chile

1 bay leaf

4 tablespoons/60 ml expeller-pressed
    avocado oil, divided

1 small red onion, sliced lengthwise
    ½ inch/12 mm thick

1 tablespoon unsalted butter

Artisanal sea salt and freshly ground
    black pepper

Finely grated zest of 1 lemon

8 small fresh hyssop leaves, or 4 each
    small fresh sage and mint leaves

Petals from 3 hyssop flowers (optional)

To make the dressing, on a cutting board, smash the garlic confit with the side of a chef's knife, then transfer it to a small bowl. Add the olive oil, lemon juice, and honey and whisk well. Season with salt and pepper and set aside.

Slice the mushrooms in half lengthwise, then score them on the cut surface to keep them from curling as they cook.

In a saucepan, combine the potatoes, water to cover generously, enough kosher salt for the water to taste moderately salty, the peppercorns, chile, and bay leaf. Bring to a boil over medium-high heat, reduce the heat to medium, and simmer until the potatoes are tender when pierced with a thin knife blade or cake tester, being careful not to break them up. The timing will depend on their size. Drain well into a colander and transfer to a cutting board. Using the side of a chef's knife, smash the potatoes gently. They should break open a little but maintain their structure.

Heat a large cast-iron or enameled-cast-iron frying pan over medium-high until quite hot. Add 2 tablespoons of the avocado oil, and when it is hot, add the mushrooms, scored side down, and sear for 2 minutes. Add the onion, flip the mushrooms over, and add the butter. Continue to cook until the butter browns and the onion is charred, about 3 minutes. Season with sea salt and pepper, transfer to a plate, and keep warm.

Line a large plate with paper towels. Heat the same pan used to cook the mushrooms over medium-high. Add the remaining 2 tablespoons avocado oil, and when it is hot, add the potatoes and sear on both sides until crispy, about 4 minutes on each side. Transfer to the plate and season with sea salt and pepper.

To serve, place 3 potatoes on each plate and arrange a mushroom half and some of the onion next to each potato. Drizzle with the dressing and garnish with the lemon zest, a couple of hyssop leaves, and a sprinkling of hyssop petals.

Bejeweled Patatas Bravas with Toasted Garlic and Tomato Sauce

Our spin on this classic Spanish tapa brings together the flavors of crispy potatoes and garlic, pungent and creamy garlic aïoli, and zesty tomato sauce. This "bejeweled" version comes from a lunch at which we served fried potatoes as a side dish. Our gardener, Colby, had just harvested a big tub of potatoes of multiple varieties. As we served them, we paused, transfixed by their vivid hues of golden topaz, amethyst, and ruby. Of course, you can make these potatoes with a single variety, but you won't feel quite as royal. This recipe calls for waxy potatoes, such as Red Bliss, Rose Finn, Carola, or Adirondack Blue. —Mike

Toasted Garlic and Tomato Sauce

6 tablespoons/90 ml extra-virgin olive oil

4 cloves garlic, thinly sliced

Artisanal sea salt

3 fresh thyme sprigs

1 bay leaf

1 small yellow onion, thinly sliced

1/2 green chile, such as Anaheim or Hatch (New Mexico), halved, seeded, and thinly sliced

1/2 teaspoon sweet smoked Spanish paprika

1 can (14 oz/440 g) organic whole tomatoes, with the juice

Aïoli

1 extra-large egg yolk from a very fresh egg, at room temperature

1 large clove garlic

Small pinch of artisanal sea salt

1/2 cup/125 ml extra-virgin olive oil

Squeeze of fresh lemon juice

Very small pinch of cayenne pepper

Bejeweled Potatoes

3 lb/1.5 kg waxy potatoes, in a mix of varieties and colors

Kosher salt

1 cup/250 ml expeller-pressed sunflower, grapeseed, or other neutral vegetable oil

Artisanal sea salt

Sweet smoked Spanish paprika for garnish

To make the sauce, in a small saucepan over medium-low heat, warm together the olive oil and garlic and cook the garlic, stirring gently, until just slightly golden, about 2 minutes. Remove from the heat. Using a slotted spoon, quickly scoop the garlic from the oil onto a paper towel. Season the garlic "chips" with salt and set aside.

Return the pan with the garlic-infused oil to medium heat and toss in the thyme sprigs and bay leaf. Once the herbs crackle in the hot oil, add the onion and a generous pinch of salt and cook, stirring occasionally, until soft and lightly browned, about 10 minutes. Add the chile and paprika and cook, stirring occasionally, for 5 minutes longer.

Scoop the tomatoes into the pan and cook at a lively simmer, breaking them up with a wooden spoon, until a sauce with a "jammy" consistency forms, about 15 minutes. Remove from the heat and let cool slightly. Remove and discard the thyme and bay, then transfer the contents of the pan to a food processor or blender and purée to a smooth consistency, taking care to cover the machine lid with a thick kitchen towel to avoid getting burned. Alternatively, pass the sauce through a food mill fitted with the fine disk. Taste the sauce and add salt if needed. Set aside and keep warm.

(continued)

Bejeweled Patatas Bravas with Toasted Garlic and Tomato Sauce (continued)

To make the aïoli, place the egg yolk in a bowl. Using a Microplane or other fine-rasp grater, grate the garlic over the egg yolk, then add the salt. Using a whisk, break up the yolk, briefly incorporating the garlic and salt. Pour the oil into a liquid measuring cup. Whisking in a slow, steady whipping-stirring motion with one hand, with your other hand start dribbling the olive oil, a few drops at a time, into the yolk mixture. You are starting an emulsion of the oil into the yolk, and if you go too fast at the beginning, you run the risk of the aïoli separating, leaving it greasy and unappealing. As you continue, you'll see that the emulsion is succeeding and the aïoli will begin to become thick and creamy. At this point, you can start whisking in the oil more quickly and continue until all the oil has been incorporated. Whisk in the lemon juice and cayenne, then taste and adjust the seasoning with salt and lemon juice if needed. Cover with plastic wrap and leave at room temperature if using within 1 hour; otherwise, refrigerate for up to 24 hours.

To prepare the potatoes, separate the different varieties, then peel and cut into pieces about 1 inch/2.5 cm square. Line a sheet pan with a few layers of paper towels. Scoop each potato variety into its own small saucepan, add water to cover, and generously season with kosher salt. Each potato variety will have its own cooking time, hence all the fuss here with the separate pans. Bring the potatoes to a lively simmer over medium heat and cook until tender, 10–15 minutes. The potatoes must be thoroughly cooked so they will develop a crisp, delicate crust when fried. If they are not simmered long enough, they will form a tough, soggy crust. Drain the cooked potatoes gently but thoroughly, then spread them in a single layer on the sheet pan.

Select a cast-iron or enameled-cast-iron frying pan large enough to hold the potatoes in a single layer. (If you don't have a pan large enough, fry the potatoes in two batches, using half the oil for each batch.) Line a sheet pan with a few layers of paper towels. Place the frying pan over medium-high heat, pour in the vegetable oil, and heat until a piece of potato dropped into the oil sizzles on contact. Add the potatoes and stir gently so they settle evenly in the pan. Fry the potatoes, stirring frequently, until golden brown and quite crispy, about 5 minutes. Using a slotted spoon or wire skimmer, carefully scoop the fried potatoes onto the sheet pan. Season with sea salt and top with a generous pinch of paprika.

To serve, spoon the warm tomato sauce onto a serving platter. Mound the potatoes on the sauce, then spoon dollops of aïoli randomly on top. Garnish the potatoes with the reserved garlic chips and add a final dusting of paprika.

TOMATOES
& PEPPERS

THE SADDEST DAY OF THE CULINARY YEAR OCCURS when we finish the last jar of fermented red pepper paste. From late summer into fall, numerous jars of the paste sit on our kitchen counter waiting for the daily stirring. Once fermentation has run its course, we pack the paste into smaller jars and store them in the walk-in refrigerator. Spicy and slightly sour with a bass note of fermented tang, this is my go-to flavoring for scrambled eggs or avocado toast. If you attempt only one recipe from this chapter, make this the one.

The second-saddest day comes when the last jar of superconcentrated tomato *conserva* is empty. The yield of *conserva* on ten pounds/five kilos of tomatoes is only a few jars. A tablespoon of this concentrate deepens and transforms a pot of soup or a slow-cooked braise.

When you have red pepper paste and tomato *conserva* in your larder, you find yourself using them with abandon. The robust earthiness of the paste and the rich umami of the *conserva* create a bridge to wine, especially aged reds. A stew, for instance, with a healthy dollop of *conserva* tastes richer and meatier, which loosens up the flavor of a full-bodied Cabernet Sauvignon.

RECIPES

The roasted pepper flavor and slight funkiness of the ferment mellows the tannins of the wine.

Late summer means boxes and boxes of tomatoes and peppers coming into the kitchen. We feature them on all our menus during this abundant season on the farm, but, believe it or not, we preserve most of the bounty.

The most basic form of preservation is drying. In the case of chiles, this could be as simple as air-drying strings of peppers in the barn or loading up the dehydrator. To dry tomatoes requires a little more prep. Canning them whole or making Tomato-Vegetable Juice (page 144) for the larder usually takes place one day in late summer when Colby brings us an especially large batch. Making tomato *conserva* requires an all-out effort. At the height of tomato season we process a hundred pounds/fifty kilos of tomatoes a week, which yields only four to five

quart or liter jars of *conserva*. As summer slowly gives way to fall, the pepper deliveries seem to pick up velocity. We feverishly try to keep up, starting multiple fermentation batches every day and hoping the end of the season is close. It's a happy problem to have.

All this talk about preserved tomatoes and peppers may give you the impression we don't like them in the fresh state. Not true. Clear, pale yellow tomato "water" is something we often serve during canapé receptions before dinners. Tomato salads abound on most of our summer and early fall menus. I haven't met too many chefs who are in love with uncooked bell peppers of any color, but we do love them grilled over a wood fire and peeled. Grilled or roasted peppers also find their way into sauces and salads, or we stuff them with rice and bake them. We blister the delicate Padrón and shishito peppers in a hot skillet and serve them whole, usually as finger food. —*John*

In the summer months, it seems that most of our gardens at Stone Edge Farm are planted to tomatoes and peppers. If you also count potatoes and eggplant, the other major members of the Solanaceae, or nightshade, family, you've got a solid majority. Summer in our microclimate can be on the cooler side, but the season is long and hot enough to successfully grow all but the slowest-ripening peppers. Small to midsize tomatoes do really well for us, too.

Harvest starts in earnest for us toward the end of July. We hit peak production around mid-September. From then it's a slow decline until the first of November. The actual end of the season for a given garden bed usually comes while it is still producing. Calling it quits is a challenging decision when fruit is still trickling off the vine, but we need space to get our fall and winter crops off to a healthy start by early October.

All our tomatoes and peppers are started from seed in a small greenhouse. We are blessed with access to a dizzying variety of types to choose from. In addition to saving our own seed, in the winter the chefs and I pore over seed catalogs from suppliers such as Baker Creek Heirloom Seeds, Seed Savers Exchange, and Johnny's Selected Seeds. We seek out funky, flavorful heirlooms, and sometimes a new hybrid will pique our interest. We also stay in touch with local breeders and growers, like Brad Gates of Wild Boar Farms, who introduces delicious and colorful new tomato varieties every year. When you plant a wide selection of such versatile crops, abundance and diversity in the garden translate to exciting results in the kitchen.

I've listed some of the varieties that typically make up the core of our plantings. Even with all these favorites, we still set aside space to try new varieties each year, and we invariably add at least a couple of new favorites to the must-grow list. —*Colby*

TOMATOES (*grouped by color*)
Black/Purple: Vorlon, Paul Robeson,
    Black Krim
Red: Red Pear Piriform, Early Girl,
    Granadero, Cuore di Bue
Yellow: Earl of Edgecombe, Jaune Flamme
Cherry: Sungold, Matt's Wild Cherry, Juliet
Striped: Green Zebra, Tigerella, Ananas Noire

PEPPERS (*grouped by culinary use*)
Frying: Shishito, Padrón, Jimmy Nardello
Hot: Rezha Macedonian, Lemon Drop, Fish
Sweet: Stocky Red Roaster, Cornito Giallo
Drying: Espelette, Aleppo, Guajillo

Tomato-Vegetable Juice

Packing summer's bounty into a refreshing drink resonates with us. This recipe is a nod to the ever-popular V8 juice. Our V12 is loaded with so much garden goodness that we think of it as a nourishing food as much as a beverage. —Mike

---

2 tablespoons extra-virgin olive oil

1 tablespoon coriander seeds

1 teaspoon fennel pollen (see page 68) (optional)

1 teaspoon fennel seeds

1 teaspoon yellow mustard seeds

1/2 teaspoon sweet paprika

1 bay leaf

3 celery ribs, thinly sliced

3 cloves garlic, sliced

1 red onion, thinly sliced

1 carrot, peeled and thinly sliced

1 fennel bulb, halved, cored, outer layer removed, and thinly sliced

1 jalapeño chile, thinly sliced

1 Anaheim or other mild green chile, seeded and thinly sliced

1 Gypsy, bell, or other sweet red pepper, seeded and thinly sliced

1 tablespoon artisanal sea salt

6 lb/3 kg vine-ripened tomatoes, cored and quartered

Small handful fresh basil leaves

6 fresh cilantro sprigs, large stems removed and roughly chopped

5 fresh flat-leaf parsley sprigs, large stems removed and roughly chopped

5 tablespoons/80 ml fresh lemon juice

Equipment

Food mill

Four 1-pt/500-l widemouthed canning jars with lids and screw bands

Large canning or similar pot with lid and wire rack

In a large, nonreactive pot over medium heat, warm the olive oil, coriander seeds, fennel pollen, fennel seeds, mustard seeds, paprika, and bay leaf, stirring once or twice, until fragrant, about 1 minute. Add the celery, garlic, onion, carrot, fennel bulb, jalapeño, Anaheim, Gypsy pepper, and salt and stir well. Cover and cook, stirring occasionally, until all the vegetables are very soft, about 15 minutes. Uncover, stir in the tomatoes, raise the heat to medium-high, and bring the mixture to a simmer. Cook uncovered, stirring occasionally, until the tomatoes are juicy and soft, about 15 minutes. Remove and discard the bay leaf, then stir in the basil, cilantro, and parsley.

Remove from the heat. Using a food mill fitted with the fine disk, carefully pass the hot mixture through the mill into a large heatproof bowl, pressing as much of the mixture through the mill as possible. Stir in the lemon juice. Clean the pot and return the tomato juice to it.

Wash the canning jars and lids in hot, soapy water. Rinse, then immerse the jars in gently boiling water for 10 minutes. Just before filling, remove the jars from the hot water and shake off any excess. Have the lids and screw bands ready.

Bring the tomato juice to a boil over high heat. Ladle the hot juice into the jars, leaving 1/2-inch/12-mm headspace, and wipe any spills from the rim with a damp towel. Cap each jar with a lid and twist on a screw band, tightening gently with just your fingertips. (Overtightening the lids prevents air in the jar from escaping during processing, which is critical to safe shelf-stable canning.) Put any juice that does not fit in the jars in an airtight container, store in the refrigerator, and use within a week or so.

Place the wire rack in the bottom of the canning pot and set the jars, not touching, on the rack. Fill the pot with water, covering the jars by about 3 inches/7.5 cm. Cover the pot, bring to a boil over high heat, and boil for 20 minutes.

Carefully transfer the jars to a work surface and let cool completely on a rack or kitchen towel. Then check for a good seal by loosening the screw bands and pressing on the center of each lid. If the lid remains concave and does not move, the seal is good. Store the jars in a cool, dark place for up to 1 year. If a jar failed to seal properly, store it in the refrigerator and use the juice within a week or so.

FERMENTED RED PEPPER PASTE AND POWDER

MAKES THREE 1-PT/500-ML JARS PASTE
AND 3 OZ/85 G POWDER

This paste and powder are must-have larder items for anyone who likes a kick of spice. The recipe will first yield four jars of the paste, one of which will then be made into the powder. Together, they will enhance your cooking throughout the year by adding an incredible depth of flavor. To prevent the pain of volatile capsicum oil penetrating the pores of your hands, it's smart to wear disposable gloves when working with a quantity of chile peppers. How many sweet versus hot peppers to use depends on your personal threshold for chile spice. —Mike

---

4 lb/2 kg mixed sweet and hot peppers, stemmed

6 cloves garlic, sliced

3 large shallots, sliced

¼ cup/65 g artisanal sea salt

EQUIPMENT

Three 1-pt/500-ml canning jars with lids and screw bands

Dehydrator (optional but highly recommended)

1 silica desiccant packet (optional)

CHEF'S NOTE:

Although not essential, a silica desiccant packet, available online, will help keep the powder dry. If air-drying the paste, make sure the cheesecloth does not touch it.

To make the paste, working in batches combine the ingredients in a blender or food processor and purée. Let the machine run for a couple of minutes to achieve as smooth a paste as possible. Pour the paste into a large, nonreactive airtight container, such as a jar with a lid, allowing at least 2 inches/5 cm headspace for the paste to expand as it ferments. Cover the paste with plastic wrap, pressing it directly onto the surface, then seal the container with its lid.

Place the container in a cupboard away from heat and light and allow to ferment, replacing the plastic wrap and stirring the paste once daily for 5 days. After 5 days, smell the fermented paste, which should have a pungent tang, and taste for mild sourness. If the paste is not pungent enough, let it ferment for another day or two, giving it a stir and continuing to change the plastic wrap daily.

When the paste is ready, wash the jars and lids in hot, soapy water. Rinse, then immerse the jars in gently boiling water for 10 minutes. Just before filling, remove the jars from the hot water and shake off any excess. Have the lids and screw bands ready.

Pack three-fourths of the paste into the jars. Let them cool to room temperature, then cap, twist on a screw band, and store in the refrigerator. The paste will keep for up to a year.

To make the powder, line 2 dehydrator trays or 2 sheet pans with silicone baking mats or parchment paper. Spread the remaining red pepper paste evenly on the trays or pans. You can dry the paste in the dehydrator at 110°F/50°C for 6 hours; or, to dry it in full sunshine, cover the trays or pans with cheesecloth to protect from insects, secure the cloth with clothespins or duct tape to hold it taut, and leave for 8–10 hours. The paste should be quite dry and crumbly. Let cool, transfer to a blender, and process until reduced to a powder, taking care not to inhale any of it.

Thoroughly wash and dry a small glass jar. Transfer the powder to the jar, add the silica desiccant packet, cap tightly, and store at room temperature for up to 1 month.

Chile Spice Mix

For this spice mix I use ancho chiles, whose sweet and smoky flavor adds depth to many dishes. Ancho chiles are green poblanos that have been dried. They should be somewhat soft and pliable. We like using this blend with pork or sprinkling it over vegetables. —Fiorella

---

1 tablespoon dried oregano

1 teaspoon coriander seeds

10 ancho chiles, seeded

1 tablespoon artisanal sea salt

EQUIPMENT

Spice mill

In a small sauté pan over medium heat, toast the oregano, coriander, and chiles, stirring often, until fragrant, 3–4 minutes. Remove from the heat and cool. Grind the oregano and coriander to a fine powder in the spice mill. Pour into a small bowl.

In a food processor, grind the chiles until reduced to flakes. Transfer them to the spice mill and grind to a fine powder. Add the chile powder to the oregano and coriander, add the salt, and stir to mix well. Transfer to a glass jar, cap tightly, and store at room temperature for up to 2 months.

Dried Cherry Tomatoes

We dry tomatoes in summer and use them throughout the year. They go into many recipes and enhance countless broths and sauces. —Fiorella

---

1 lb/500 g cherry tomatoes, stemmed

EQUIPMENT

Dehydrator (optional)

1-pt/500-ml glass jar with lid

CHEF'S NOTE:

If you prefer a softer tomato texture, cut the dehydrating or oven time by a few hours. These softer tomatoes will be more perishable, however. To store, transfer to the jar, add olive oil to cover, and refrigerate.

Cut the tomatoes in half and arrange, cut sides up, in a snug single layer on a dehydrator tray. Dry the tomatoes at 130°F/55°C until fully dried, 10–12 hours. If you do not have a dehydrator, preheat the oven to the lowest setting (150°F/65°C). Line a sheet pan with a silicone baking mat or with parchment paper, overlapping it on all sides. Arrange the tomatoes, cut sides up, in a snug single layer on the pan and bake overnight. Be sure to crowd the tomatoes together because they will shrink as they dry and the space around them will grow. After drying or baking the tomatoes, let them cool completely before filling the jar.

Wash the jar and lid in hot, soapy water. Rinse, shake off the water, and set the jar and lid aside to dry completely.

Spoon the dried tomatoes into the jar. Cap with the lid and store in a cool, dry place for up to 8 months.

TOMATO CONSERVA

Homemade tomato conserva bears little similarity to commercially prepared tomato paste, even the imported stuff from Italy. It is the very essence of tomato in a superconcentrated form. Just one spoonful of conserva will make a minestrone soup taste like an Italian grandmother stepped into your kitchen. To rekindle a memory of Spain, spoon a thin layer on toasted garlic bread and drizzle it with olive oil for an astounding pan con tomate. You will need what may seem like a lot of tomatoes to make two small jars of this precious condiment. Paste tomatoes, such as Roma or plum types, will give you the thickest conserva, but any vine-ripened tomatoes will work. —Mike

---

10 lb/5 kg ripe tomatoes

1 teaspoon artisanal sea salt

Extra-virgin olive oil for pans and to top off jars

EQUIPMENT

Food mill or chinois (fine-mesh conical sieve)

Two ½-pt/250-ml glass jars with lids

Cut large tomatoes into quarters, and cut medium and small tomatoes into halves. Don't worry about stems and cores, as they will be removed later. Put all the tomatoes in a large, heavy nonreactive pot and add the salt. Place over high heat and cook, stirring frequently with a wooden spoon to ensure nothing sticks to the pot bottom, until the tomatoes boil and release their juices, about 10 minutes.

Position oven racks in the center and top third of the oven and preheat the oven to 250°F/135°C. Using the food mill fitted with the fine disk or a chinois, carefully pass the hot tomatoes through the mill or sieve into a large bowl. Coat 2 large sheet pans with the olive oil, then divide the puréed tomatoes evenly between them.

Place the pans in the oven. After 1 hour, pull the pans from the oven and use a rubber spatula or, better yet, a baker's dough scraper to fold the mixture onto itself. It is especially important to scrape the edges of the pans, where the sauce will evaporate first. Return the pans to the oven. Repeat the scraping and folding every 30 minutes until the mixture has significantly reduced in volume, about 3 hours. Then combine the mixture from both pans onto a single pan and continue baking until the mixture is a glossy brick red and as thick as tomato paste. This last step should take about 3 more hours. Remove from the oven and let cool to room temperature.

Wash the jars and lids in hot, soapy water. Rinse, then immerse the jars in gently boiling water for 10 minutes. Carefully remove the jars from the hot water and shake off any excess. Have the lids ready.

Pack the conserva into the jars with a tablespoon, leaving ½-inch/12-mm headspace, and top off with a thin film of olive oil. Cap each jar with a lid and store in the refrigerator for up to 1 year.

Charred Padrón Peppers with Goat Cheese and Sage

Blistering Padrón peppers over high heat with oil and salt results in one of the culinary world's great alchemical transformations. In this version, earthy sage leaves and goat cheese add a satisfying twist to the peppers. While testing this recipe at home, I discovered that the only goat cheese in the house was frozen solid. After letting it thaw a bit on the kitchen counter, I decided not to wait and grated a blanket of snowy goat cheese over the hot Padróns. Not for the first time, I made a delightful discovery born out of necessity. —John

2 oz/60 g fresh goat cheese

2½ teaspoons extra-virgin olive oil

½ lb/375 g Padrón or shishito peppers, stems intact

16 fresh sage leaves

1 teaspoon artisanal sea salt

Place the goat cheese in the freezer for 30 minutes before you begin to cook the peppers.

Heat a 12-inch/30-cm cast-iron or carbon-steel frying pan over high heat. When the pan is very hot, add the oil and swirl to coat the bottom of the pan. Add the peppers and sage leaves and immediately begin constantly moving the peppers around with a wooden spatula or by jerking the pan backward toward you repeatedly to flip them. This method is similar to moving food continuously in a wok over high heat. After a few minutes, sprinkle the salt evenly over the peppers. They are ready when they began to soften and some of them have a nice char. The total cooking time will be less than 5 minutes.

Transfer the peppers to a wide, shallow bowl or platter. Using a cheese grater, shower the goat cheese evenly over the top. Because the peppers can be picked up by their stems, this is a communal dish, best eaten with the fingers.

TOMATOES & PEPPERS   157

Chilled Tomato Soup with Mussels and Fennel

On long days or warm nights, this soup works well as a light lunch or a first course for dinner. You can make it ahead and keep it in the fridge for up to twenty-four hours. If you are not a fan of mussels, you can substitute clams or shrimp. —Fiorella

1 tablespoon expeller-pressed sunflower oil

1 small yellow onion, chopped

1 small fennel bulb, halved, cored, outer layer removed, and chopped

5 cloves garlic, chopped

1 teaspoon sweet or smoked paprika

1 teaspoon ground coriander

1/2 teaspoon fennel pollen (see page 68)

1 tablespoon Tomato Conserva (page 150)

1 1/2 lb/750 g plum tomatoes, cored and chopped

2 tablespoons dry white vermouth

4 cups/1 l filtered water

2 fresh thyme sprigs

2 bay leaves

16 mussels in the shell, scrubbed and debearded

1/4 cup/60 ml dry white wine

1 serrano chile, seeds and membranes removed and finely diced

Juice of 1/2 lemon

Artisanal sea salt and freshly ground black pepper

Small edible flowers and/or cilantro leaves for garnish (optional)

Heat a saucepan over medium-low and add the sunflower oil. When the oil is hot, add the onion and chopped fennel and cook, stirring occasionally, until slightly softened, 3–4 minutes. Add the garlic, paprika, coriander, and fennel pollen and stir with a wooden spoon for about 1 minute. Add the conserva and cook, stirring, for 2 minutes longer. Add the tomatoes, raise the heat to medium, and cook, stirring occasionally, until soft, about 7 minutes. Add the vermouth and let it evaporate and integrate for about 2 minutes, then add the water, thyme, and bay leaves. Bring to a boil, lower the heat to a simmer, and cook uncovered until the liquid has reduced by about one-third, about 30 minutes.

Just before the soup is ready, fill a large bowl with ice and water and nest a medium bowl in it. Remove the soup from the heat, remove and discard the thyme sprigs and bay leaves, and season with salt and pepper. Let cool slightly, then in batches, purée the soup in a blender until smooth and pass the purée through a fine-mesh sieve into the medium bowl. Stir the soup until it cools down. You should have about 4 cups/1 l soup. Cover the bowl and chill the soup in the refrigerator until ready to serve.

In a sauté pan over medium-high heat, combine the mussels, discarding any that failed to close when touched, and the wine. Cover the pan and cook until the mussels open, 3–5 minutes. As soon as they open, pour them and their liquid into a stainless-steel bowl. Let cool slightly and then refrigerate until chilled.

Remove the mussels from the refrigerator and shell them, keeping the meats whole. Discard the shells and place the meats in a small container. Add the chile and lemon juice, mix well, cover, and return to the refrigerator if not serving right away. Strain the mussel cooking liquid through a fine-mesh sieve into the chilled soup. Taste and add salt and pepper if needed. Cover and return to the refrigerator until serving.

To serve, place 4 mussels in each bowl and pour or ladle the soup around them. Or ladle the soup tableside if you wish. Garnish each serving with the flowers.

STUFFED PEPPERS WITH BASMATI RICE

This dish was inspired by my family roots. Arequipa, the city where I lived as a child, is in southern Peru. Located at the base of three volcanoes and built with volcanic stone, Arequipa's status as a UNESCO World Heritage Site honors the rich cultural heritage of both indigenous inhabitants and immigrants from around the world. Spaniards brought this recipe to Peru. Although the peppers are traditionally stuffed with beef and served with a potato gratin, this version is vegetarian. It can be served as a tapa or first course. —Fiorella

---

¼ cup basmati rice

2 large eggs

4 small red bell or other sweet peppers

3 tablespoons extra-virgin olive oil

I red onion, finely diced

4 cloves garlic, minced

I tablespoon ground cumin

I teaspoon ground turmeric

I teaspoon Chile Spice Mix (page 149)

2 tablespoons sherry vinegar

5 Kalamata or other brine-cured black olives, pitted and halved

2 tablespoons peanuts, lightly toasted and coarsely chopped

I tablespoon golden raisins, soaked in water to cover for 10 minutes and drained

2 tablespoons unsalted butter

Artisanal sea salt and freshly ground black pepper

½ cup/60 g finely grated ricotta salata cheese, divided

½ cup Meyer Lemon Aïoli (page 42) for serving (optional)

In a small bowl, soak the rice in cold water to cover for 20 minutes, then drain into a sieve and rinse with cold running water for 10 seconds. In a small saucepan over high heat, combine the rice with water to cover by ½ inch/12 mm, bring to a boil, reduce the heat to low, cover, and cook until tender, 10–15 minutes. Uncover, fluff with a fork, and reserve uncovered.

In a small saucepan, combine the eggs with water to cover generously, bring to a gentle boil over medium-high heat, and boil for 12 minutes. Meanwhile, fill a bowl with water and ice. When the eggs are ready, carefully scoop them from the pan and plunge them into the ice water bath until cold. Peel, coarsely chop, and set aside.

Empty the bowl and refill with water and ice. Bring a large saucepan filled with water to a boil over medium-high heat. Add the peppers and blanch for 8 seconds. Using a spider or wire skimmer, transfer them to the ice water bath for I minute to cool down. Cut off the top of each pepper with a paring knife and reserve the tops for serving. Gently remove and discard the seeds from the peppers, being careful not to split the sides, and set aside.

Position a rack in the top third of the oven and preheat the oven to 375°F/190°C. In a small sauté pan over medium heat, warm the olive oil. Add the onion and cook, stirring occasionally, until translucent, about 3 minutes. Add the garlic, cumin, turmeric, and spice mix and stir for about 2 minutes. Add the vinegar and deglaze the pan, stirring to dislodge any browned bits on the pan bottom. Add the olives, peanuts, and raisins and cook, stirring frequently, for 3 minutes longer. Add the butter, let it melt, and then stir in the rice with a fork. Remove from the heat and season with salt and pepper.

Carefully stuff the peppers with the rice filling, dividing it evenly. Add chopped egg to each pepper, then top each one with 2 tablespoons of the ricotta salata. Arrange the peppers in a baking dish, place on the top rack of the oven, and bake for 5 minutes.

Serve the peppers garnished with their tops and with the aïoli on the side for spooning over them.

PANZANELLA

Making panzanella is an opportunity to showcase the myriad tomato varieties that thrive in your garden. We serve this salad in late summer, when tomatoes are most flavorful. We like how the concentrated flavor of oven-dried cherry tomatoes melts into the fresh tomatoey juices, amplifying the whole experience. If you make a double batch of the oven-dried cherry tomatoes, the extras can be kept in the fridge under olive oil. They make a great super-quick topping for crostini and are delicious tossed into a salad. —Mike

SLOW-ROASTED CHERRY TOMATOES

¹/₂ lb/250 g vine-ripened Sun Gold
    or other flavorful cherry tomatoes,
    stemmed

1 tablespoon extra-virgin olive oil

2 cloves garlic, smashed

¹/₂ teaspoon pure maple syrup

Artisanal sea salt

¹/₄ lb/125 g pain au levain or other
    artisanal bread, torn into
    1¹/₂-inch/4-cm pieces

2 tablespoons extra-virgin olive oil,
    plus ¹/₂ cup/125 ml

Artisanal sea salt and freshly ground
    black pepper

1 large shallot, finely minced

1 clove garlic, lightly smashed

2 tablespoons red wine vinegar

Large handful fresh basil leaves

2 lb/1 kg vine-ripened tomatoes,
    a mixture of varieties, cored

To slow-roast the cherry tomatoes, preheat the oven to 200°F/95°C. In a bowl, toss the tomatoes with the olive oil, garlic, maple syrup, and a generous pinch of salt, coating them evenly. Transfer the tomatoes to a baking dish and roast until the consistency is "jammy" and the tomatoes have a deep, concentrated flavor, about 3 hours. Remove from the oven and discard the garlic cloves.

In another bowl, toss the bread with 2 tablespoons of the olive oil and a pinch of sea salt and spread in a single layer on a sheet pan. Let the bread absorb the oil for about 10 minutes while the oven preheats to 425°F/220°C. Toast the bread until deep golden brown with lightly charred edges, 8–10 minutes. Remove from the oven and let cool completely.

In a small bowl, combine the shallot, garlic, vinegar, 2 or 3 of the basil leaves, and a generous pinch of salt. Allow the shallot to macerate in the vinegar mixture for 20 minutes. Remove and discard the garlic and basil, which will have perfumed the vinegar mixture.

Cut the ripe tomatoes into big wedges or cubes and scoop into a large bowl. Add the roasted cherry tomatoes, the shallot mixture, and the remaining ¹/₂ cup/125 ml olive oil and season with salt and pepper. Tear the remaining basil leaves into the bowl, then toss the salad gently with a big spoon. Allow the tomatoes to sit and give off their juices for about 15 minutes. About 5 minutes before you plan to serve the salad, stir in the toasted bread and to allow it to absorb some of the juices while still maintaining some crunch.

Green Beans with Roasted Peppers and Shallots

SERVES 4–6

Late summer brings an abundance of peppers, which we preserve by fermenting into a paste that we use liberally throughout the year. We begin the process by building a fire outside on our grill, and when oak turns to ember we roast the peppers until they are slightly blackened and soft. Next they go into a covered container for fifteen minutes so the skins can be easily removed. During the season of pepper harvest, these fire-roasted peppers find their way into much of our cooking, as in this recipe with green beans from the farm. A bit of fermented red pepper paste adds a touch of heat, and dried cherry tomatoes provide extra crunch. —John

---

4 Corno di Toro or red bell peppers or a mixture of sweet peppers, roasted, peeled, seeded, and cut into narrow strips

3 teaspoons extra-virgin olive oil, divided

1 teaspoon fresh lemon juice

Artisanal sea salt and freshly ground black pepper

Kosher salt

³⁄₄ lb/375 g green beans, ends trimmed

1 large shallot, thinly sliced

2 cloves garlic, thinly sliced

2 teaspoons Fermented Red Pepper Paste (page 147)

2 tablespoons Dried Cherry Tomatoes (page 149), coarsely chopped

In a bowl, toss the peppers with 1 teaspoon of the olive oil, the lemon juice, ¹⁄₄ teaspoon sea salt, and a few grinds of pepper. Set aside.

Have ready a sheet pan. Bring a large pot filled with water to a boil over high heat, salt it generously with kosher salt, add the beans, and cook until crisp-tender, 1¹⁄₂–2 minutes. Using a wire skimmer, scoop out the beans and spread them in a single layer on the sheet pan to cool until ready to finish the dish.

Heat a 12-inch/30-cm sauté pan over medium-low. When the pan is hot, add the remaining 2 teaspoons olive oil, the shallot, garlic, and ¹⁄₄ teaspoon sea salt and cook, stirring with a wooden spoon, until the shallot softens, 2–3 minutes. Raise the heat to medium-high, add the pepper paste and dried tomatoes, and stir vigorously to combine. Add the beans and ³⁄₄ teaspoon sea salt and cook, stirring, until the beans are mixed with the other ingredients and heated through, about 1 minute longer.

To serve, arrange the beans on a platter and top with the reserved peppers.

FIGS &
QUINCES

I WAS TEACHING A COOKING CLASS AT A MIDDLE SCHOOL in their vegetable garden one bright fall morning. The garden contained various pome fruit trees, including apples, pears, and a lone quince, whose fruit I planned to add to a roasted butternut squash soup. As I peeled and chopped it, I explained to the mostly Hispanic students that quince is the only fruit you can't eat raw. My hubris was immediately challenged by a student who informed me that his family ate raw shaved quince with chile powder, lime juice, and salt. Five minutes later, with this flavor combination in mind, we tucked into a delicious plate of *membrillo con chile y limón* with chile powder from our larder at Edge and limes from the Stone Edge Farm orchard. I was reminded why I love to teach young people about food. I learn so much!

RECIPES

With its tropical fruity perfume, ripe quince quickly fills any space with an alluring aroma. Despite my lesson about eating it raw, quince reveals its true personality when it is cooked. The fruit has an irregular bumpy shape and fuzzy skin surrounding a very hard interior. The transformation from pale yellow raw quince to rosy-pink *membrillo* is truly astonishing. *Membrillo* is a regular feature on our cheese plates. It pairs especially well with dry aged cheeses, such as Manchego, cheddar, and *pecorino toscano*, and with red wine.

Quinces and figs arrive in our kitchen at the same time in early fall. Although no recipes requiring fig leaves appear in this chapter, we regularly use them to wrap goat cheese or fish before grilling or baking. They can be substituted for grape leaves. The fig leaf imparts a fruity nuttiness to food and, when grilled, an appealing smoky flavor.

Fig trees bear two crops. The first crop, in early summer, is the breba figs. These pale in comparison to the sweeter and more succulent main crop in late summer and early autumn. The popular Black Mission variety grows so abundantly around Sonoma that most folks would never dream of going to the store to buy them. The other varieties we cultivate at Stone Edge Farm include the Green Ischia, pale green on the outside and bright red on the inside when ripe, and the exotic, variegated Green Tiger Stripe.

A perfectly ripe and jammy fig still warm from the tree has inspired many a painter and poet, but I believe most figs reach their full potential with the application of some heat. Prosciutto-wrapped griddled figs make an easy canapé. Jam made from figs and fennel pollen (page 180) provides inspiration for salad dressings and cheese plates and serves as the base for our sweet and savory Fig Anchoïade (page 182). —*John*

QUINCE VINEGAR

Fruit vinegar is fun to make and tastes less sharp than wine vinegar. You can use it in salads, gastriques, and sauces. On visits to Cuzco, Peru, I enjoy a popular drink called frutillada, *which uses fresh strawberries fermented into a low-alcohol wine. Adding a "mother" of unfiltered vinegar turns the wine into acetic acid, but the fruit wine will acidify even without it. I chose quince for this recipe, but nearly any fruit in season will work. —Fiorella*

---

2 lb/1 kg quinces, unpeeled, halved, cored, and chopped

½ cup/105 g firmly packed organic light brown sugar

8 cups/2 l water

¼ cup/60 ml vinegar starter, such as unfiltered apple cider vinegar with the mother

EQUIPMENT

1-gal/4-l widemouthed glass jar with lid

2-qt/2-l widemouthed glass jar

Cheesecloth, about 6 inches/15 cm square

Kitchen twine or large rubber band

Two 1-qt/1-l bottles with lids

Wash the 1-gal/4-l jar and lid in hot, soapy water. Rinse, shake off the water, and let the jar and lid dry completely.

Put the quinces in the jar. There should be at least 1-qt/1-l headspace to allow for proper fermentation.

In a bowl or pitcher, add the sugar to the water and stir well to dissolve. Add the sugar water to the jar with the quinces and wipe any spills from the rim with a damp cloth. Cap the jar with the lid. Let stand at cool room temperature (60°F–70°F/15°C–/21°C). Unseal the jar every other day to release the gas and then reseal. The quince wine is ready when it tastes tangy. The timing will vary depending on room temperature and humidity. Allow about 2 weeks.

Wash the 2-qt/2-l jar in hot, soapy water. Rinse, shake off all the water, and let the jar dry completely.

Pass the quince mixture through a fine-mesh sieve into the jar. Add the vinegar starter. Cover the jar with the cheesecloth to allow fermentation and secure with kitchen twine or a rubber band. Keep the jar at room temperature in a cupboard or other dark place. Taste the vinegar every week until the acidity develops to your liking. It usually takes about 2 months but can take up to 3–4 months.

Transfer the vinegar to the bottles and seal tightly. Store out of the light at room temperature and allow the vinegar to age until it is to your liking. The longer the vinegar sits, the more rounded it will taste, from 2–3 months up to 6 months.

CHEESE BOARD WITH QUINCE PASTE

At Edge, we love serving cheeses that complement and elevate our wines. Putting together a cheese board is also a way we feature items from our larder. You can choose different types of cheeses, as the color, texture, and milk from different animals creates an interesting presentation. Fresh seasonal fruit, dried fruit, fruit pastes, and honey all enhance the experience. —Fiorella

---

½ cup/60 g walnut halves

½ cup/85 g almonds

Leaves from 2 fresh thyme sprigs

1 teaspoon expeller-pressed avocado oil

Artisanal sea salt and freshly ground
black pepper

1 baguette

Fig leaves for serving (optional)

1 wedge Garrotxa or other semifirm
goat's milk cheese, about ½ lb/250 g

1 wedge Cabot Clothbound or other aged
Cheddar cheese, about ½ lb/250 g

1 wedge San Andreas or
other hard sheep's milk cheese,
about ½ lb/250 g

¼ lb/125 g Quince Paste (page 177),
cut into small cubes

8 ripe figs, stemmed and halved
lengthwise

1 cup/140 g Oven-Dried Grapes
(page 225), or a large cluster of
fresh grapes

Preheat the oven to 350°F/180°C. Line a small sheet pan with parchment paper.

In a small bowl, combine the walnuts, almonds, and thyme. Drizzle with the avocado oil, season with salt and pepper, and toss to coat evenly. Spread the nuts in a single layer on the sheet pan and place in the oven until lightly toasted and fragrant, 6–7 minutes. Transfer the pan to a wire rack to cool.

When ready to serve, cut the baguette into slices ½ inch/12 mm thick and place in a basket. If using the fig leaves, arrange them, overlapping one another, on one side of a wooden board or platter. Place the cheese wedges on the leaves. Put the nuts in the middle of the board or platter and arrange the quince paste, figs, and grapes next to them. Serve the bread alongside.

Fig and Fennel Pollen Jam

Fig jam is a wonderfully versatile pantry item to reach for throughout the year. The fact that it isn't too sweet makes it a good condiment for savory dishes such as roast pork. It's equally good to spread over your favorite whole-grain toast. Wild fennel pollen imparts the delicate flavor of anise, which complements the figs' earthiness. —Mike

---

6 oz/185 g shallots
 (about 4 medium-large), unpeeled

½ teaspoon expeller-pressed vegetable
 oil, such as sunflower or grapeseed

2 lb/1 kg ripe figs, stemmed and
 quartered lengthwise

½ cup/125 ml water

2 tablespoons honey

2 tablespoons organic sugar

½ teaspoon fennel pollen
 (see page 68), or 1 teaspoon
 ground fennel seeds

Pinch of artisanal sea salt

1 tablespoon fresh lemon juice

Equipment

Glass jars and lids

Wash enough jars and lids in hot, soapy water to accommodate the jam. Rinse, shake off the water, and set the jars and lids aside to dry completely.

Preheat the oven to 425°F/220°C.

Put the shallots in a small baking dish, toss with the oil, then cover the dish with aluminum foil and roast the shallots until soft, 15–20 minutes. Let cool, then peel and coarsely chop.

In a heavy saucepan, combine the shallots, figs, water, honey, sugar, fennel pollen, and salt and bring to a boil over medium-high heat. Reduce the heat to medium and cook, stirring constantly with a wooden spoon, until thick and glossy, about 15 minutes.

Remove from the heat, stir in the lemon juice, and spoon into the jars. Let cool to room temperature, then cap the jars with the lids. Store the jam in the refrigerator for up to 1 month.

Fig Anchoïade

MAKES ABOUT 1⅓ CUPS/420 G

A staple in Provence, anchoïade *is nothing more than anchovies, garlic, and olive oil worked together with a mortar and pestle into a purée. At Edge we've added walnuts and ripe, earthy figs to create a bold, sweet, and savory spread for toasted slices of rustic country bread or crackers, or a condiment for grilled swordfish. If you stock your larder with our Fig and Fennel Pollen Jam, throwing together a batch of this incredible treat is super easy. —Mike*

½ cup/60 g walnut halves

4–5 olive oil–packed anchovy fillets

2 cloves garlic

Leaves from 2 fresh thyme sprigs, chopped

¼ teaspoon artisanal sea salt

I cup/315 g Fig and Fennel Pollen Jam (page 180)

¼ cup/60 ml extra-virgin olive oil

I ½ teaspoons sherry vinegar

Freshly ground black pepper

High-quality whole-grain crackers, for serving

Equipment

Mortar and pestle

Preheat the oven or toaster oven to 350°F/180°C. Spread the walnuts in a single layer in a small, shallow pan and toast until lightly browned and fragrant, 4–5 minutes. Transfer the pan to a wire rack to cool.

Using the mortar and pestle, pound together the anchovies, garlic, thyme, and salt to a smooth paste. Add the walnuts and pound briefly just until coarsely ground. Stir in the jam, olive oil, and vinegar and season with a few grinds of pepper. Taste and adjust the seasoning with salt if needed.

The anchoïade is best the same day it is made, but it can be enjoyed for up to 3 days if covered and kept refrigerated. Bring to room temperature before serving.

CHEF'S NOTE:

Commercially prepared fig preserves may be substituted for the Fig and Fennel Pollen Jam.

Quince has an affinity for many foods, pork being at the front of the line. Grilling the chops over oak embers imbues them with a deep and smoky flavor. I like to cook meat on a Tuscan grill, which is simply a cast-iron cooking grate with two handles that rests on an open metal stand. The fire burns right on the ground. The goal of building a hardwood fire is to create a bed of embers, which are the glowing coals of a dying fire. It requires a substantial amount of wood. —John

4 bone-in center-cut pork chops, each about 1 inch/2.5 cm thick

3 teaspoons artisanal sea salt, divided

Freshly ground black pepper

2 shallots, sliced

2 cloves garlic, sliced

Juice of 1 lemon, plus 1 lemon, sliced

1/3 cup/80 ml extra-virgin olive oil

3 tablespoons dry white wine

2 teaspoons dried oregano, preferably Greek

2 teaspoons chopped fresh rosemary leaves

2 teaspoons ground Aleppo chile or piment d'Espelette

2 teaspoons firmly packed organic light brown sugar

Quince Mostarda (page 176)

One day before serving, season the pork chops on both sides with 2 teaspoons of the salt and a few grinds of pepper. Cover loosely with aluminum foil and refrigerate.

The next day, prepare the marinade. In a small bowl, combine the shallots, garlic, lemon juice and slices, olive oil, wine, oregano, rosemary, Aleppo chile, and brown sugar and mix well. Place the pork chops in a single layer in a baking dish, pour the marinade over them, and turn them a few times to coat evenly. Cover the dish with plastic wrap and refrigerate, turning the chops a few more times, for at least 6 hours or up to overnight. Two hours before grilling, remove the chops from the marinade and bring to room temperature. Discard the marinade. Season the chops on both sides with the remaining 1 teaspoon salt and a few grinds of pepper.

Build a hot oak or other hardwood fire for direct-heat grilling, allowing at least 1 hour for the fire to burn down to the correct temperature. It is ready when a coating of white ash has formed over glowing red embers. Be sure to use plenty of fuel to ensure an adequate bed of embers. Position the grill rack about 12 inches/30 cm from the fire, let the rack heat up for 5 minutes, and then clean the grate well with a wire brush. If it is not possible to build a hardwood fire, preheat a gas grill on medium for 10 minutes, then place a griddle or plancha on the grill rack, close the grill lid, and preheat for 15 minutes. Proceed with the recipe as directed.

Arrange the chops on the rack directly over the fire and grill for 5 minutes on the first side. If a flare-up occurs, raise the grill rack a little higher. Flip the chops over and cook for 5 minutes on the second side. If you prefer slightly pink pork, test for doneness by poking the center of a chop with your fingertip; if it feels a little springy, it is ready. If you prefer your pork well done, cook for a few minutes longer on each side.

Transfer the chops to a platter and let rest for 10 minutes, then cut against the grain into pieces 1 inch/2.5 cm thick. To serve, arrange the pork on a wooden platter and top with the mostarda.

Poached Quinces with Huckleberries and Crème Fraîche Ice Cream

We find plenty of uses for quinces when the harvest of this richly perfumed fruit comes in. Its versatility inspires many dishes, both savory and sweet. The wild fruity tang of huckleberries blends really well with the flavor of quince, but if you can't find huckleberries, you can omit them and still have great success. Try poaching pears in this syrup, too. —Mike

---

Crème Fraîche Ice Cream

1⅓ cups/330 ml whole milk

½ cup/100 g organic sugar

Pinch of artisanal salt

6 large egg yolks

¾ cup/180 ml heavy cream

¾ cup/185 g crème fraîche

Red Wine Poaching Syrup

1 bottle (750 ml) fruity red wine

1 cup/200 g organic sugar

½ cup/60 g huckleberries

¼ cup/60 ml water

4 whole cloves

2 lemon zest strips, ½ inch/12 mm wide

2-inch/5-cm piece vanilla bean

1-inch/2.5-cm piece cinnamon stick

2½ lb/1.25 kg quinces (about 4 large)

Equipment

Ice cream maker

To make the ice cream, fill a large bowl with ice and water. Nest a medium bowl in the ice water bath. Combine the milk, sugar, and salt in a saucepan over low heat and simmer, stirring occasionally, until the sugar dissolves. Remove from the heat. In a bowl, whisk the egg yolks until blended. Slowly pour the hot milk mixture into the egg yolks while whisking constantly. Pour the mixture back into the saucepan, place over medium-low heat, and cook, stirring constantly with a heat-resistant rubber spatula and scraping the bottom and sides as you go, until the mixture begins to thicken and coats the spatula, about 5 minutes. Whisk in the cream and crème fraîche and remove from the heat.

Pour the mixture through a fine-mesh sieve into the bowl nested in the ice water bath. Let cool, stirring occasionally, until well chilled. Pour into an ice cream maker and churn until softly frozen. Transfer to a container and store in the freezer until ready to serve. You should have about 1 qt/1 l.

To prepare the poaching syrup, combine the wine, sugar, huckleberries, water, cloves, lemon zest, vanilla bean, and cinnamon in a large pot and bring to a gentle simmer over low heat, stirring to dissolve the sugar. While the mixture is cooking, peel, halve, quarter, and core the quinces and drop them into the simmering wine mixture.

To keep the quinces submerged in the liquid, set a heatproof plate slightly smaller than the diameter of the pot on top of them, then cook over low heat until the fruit is easily pierced with a small knife, 15–30 minutes. Remove from the heat and let cool. The fruits and their poaching syrup can be stored in a covered container in the refrigerator for up to 2 weeks.

When ready to serve, use a slotted spoon to transfer the quince quarters to a cutting board. Pour 1 cup/250 ml of the poaching syrup into a small saucepan, bring to a simmer over medium heat, and cook until reduced by half and thickened slightly, about 10 minutes. Remove from the heat and let cool.

Slice the quince quarters lengthwise about ½ inch/12 mm thick and fan the slices on individual plates or shallow bowls. Place a scoop of ice cream next to the quince slices and drizzle the slices with some of the reduced syrup.

Fresh Fig Tart with Rosemary-Cornmeal Crust and Honey-Blackberry Glaze

This rustic tart celebrates the different fig varieties that ripen in our Mediterranean climate at summer's end. The fruit is layered onto a pillow of barely sweetened mascarpone set into a crisp sweet-and-savory rosemary crust. It's a stunning dessert that makes a memorable ending to a harvest feast. —Mike

Rosemary-Cornmeal Crust

1 cup/125 g plus 1 tablespoon all-purpose flour

3 tablespoons fine-grind yellow cornmeal

1/2 cup/125 g unsalted butter, at room temperature

1/3 cup/65 g organic sugar

1/4 teaspoon artisanal sea salt

1/4 teaspoon pure vanilla extract

1 large egg yolk

1 teaspoon finely chopped fresh rosemary leaves

Nonstick cooking spray for the pan

Honey-Blackberry Glaze

2 tablespoons honey

8 blackberries

Fig-Mascarpone Filling

3/4 cup/185 g mascarpone cheese, at room temperature

1/4 cup/60 g crème fraîche

2 tablespoons organic sugar

1 teaspoon finely grated lemon zest

1/4 teaspoon pure vanilla extract

Pinch of artisanal sea salt

1 lb/500 g ripe figs, stemmed and halved lengthwise

To make the crust, stir together the flour and cornmeal in a bowl. In a stand mixer fitted with the paddle attachment, combine the butter, sugar, salt, and vanilla and beat together on medium speed for about 30 seconds. Stop the machine and scrape down the sides of the bowl with a rubber spatula. Beat for 30 seconds longer, then stop the machine, add the egg yolk and rosemary, and beat briefly on medium speed just until incorporated. Stop the mixer and scrape down the sides again. Add the flour mixture and mix on low speed until all the flour mixture is moistened and the dough starts to look like crumble topping, about 15 seconds. The dough should hold together when a nugget of it is squeezed.

Use cooking spray to lightly coat a 9-inch/23-cm tart pan with a removable bottom. With lightly floured hands, press the dough evenly into the pan, applying extra pressure where the sides meet the bottom. Refrigerate for at least 30 minutes before baking.

Preheat the oven to 350°F/180°C. Bake the tart shell until deep golden brown, about 20 minutes. Let cool on a wire rack. Carefully remove the tart shell from the pan and place it on a cake stand or serving plate.

To make the glaze, combine the honey and blackberries in a small saucepan and bring to a simmer over medium heat. Simmer, stirring and gently smashing the berries with a wooden spoon, until the berries have broken down and the syrupy mixture has thickened somewhat, about 5 minutes. Pour the syrup through a fine-mesh sieve into a small heatproof bowl, pushing on the berry solids with the back of the spoon. Let the glaze cool completely.

To make the filling, combine the mascarpone, crème fraîche, sugar, lemon zest, vanilla, and salt in a bowl and stir with a wooden spoon until smooth. Gently spread the mascarpone evenly in the cooled tart shell and arrange the figs decoratively on top, cut sides up. Brush the figs with the syrup.

The tart can be prepared up to 3 hours before serving and stored uncovered at room temperature. Cut into wedges to serve.

OLIVES &

OLIVE OIL

OUR VITICULTURIST PHIL COTURRI'S CREW ARRIVES AT FIRST LIGHT on a cold November morning at Stone Edge Farm. Spreading nets under the trees heavy with fruit, they begin the ancient process of turning olives into oil. The workers strip the trees quickly and expertly before filling open-topped bins. Forklifted onto a flatbed truck, the olives don't linger for more than a few hours before we deliver them to a nearby olive mill that presses them into oil for us.

Freshly pressed olive oil, or *olio nuovo*, smells of freshly mowed grass and underripe green fruit. It is packed with antioxidants and complex polyphenols. The cloudy oil tastes peppery and bitter, though not in an unpleasant way. It will mellow and clarify with age, but we love this brash

RECITES

and vibrant youngster for its ability to wake up our palates. Unlike wine, olive oil does not improve with age, so we take steps to slow the eventual loss of quality. Storing the oil in dark-green bottles protects it from the diminishing effects of light, and caching it in an out-of-the-way corner of the wine cellar keeps it cool. After a few months, the neon-green oil has settled into a more restrained olive green and the cough-inducing peppery sensation has mellowed considerably.

Not as pungent as the Tuscan varieties, the Manzanillo olive we grow at Stone Edge Farm produces a softer, almost buttery oil that pairs very well with dishes made with our wines. Olive oil is the not-so-secret ingredient in almost everything served in our dining room at Edge. Heating high-quality (and expensive) extra-virgin olive oil to the smoking point

wouldn't make sense, but the oil doesn't reach that point for most sautéing and cooking, so we use generous amounts in our kitchen.

My first time curing green olives, I armed myself with a can of lye-based drain cleaner, long rubber gloves, and tight-fitting goggles. The olives spent a night in the same caustic solution used by commercial and many do-it-yourself olive curers. The result was an olive that after several water baths and soaks tasted more or less like commercially prepared olives: pretty good, if a little soft. After a few weeks in a brine solution, they tasted even better.

The next year I tried the water-cure method. It required a lot more work and time but resulted in a cured olive that tasted fruity. This batch, too, went into a brine solution that after some weeks produced an olive with deep flavor and a firm texture. We also began using a time-honored Palestinian method of curing green olives in a saltwater brine that supports lacto-fermentation. After several weeks the olives can be rinsed and eaten, or used in a recipe. —*John*

OLIVES IN THE GARDEN

I give a lot of garden tours at Stone Edge Farm. On any given week, the groups can range from a high school class of thirty to a couple of wine lovers from Chicago. No matter the season, there are things to taste as we make our way around the farm. We identify and smell unique herbs, nibble fresh arugula, and sample any fruits that happen to be ripe. In the late summer and fall, when our olive trees are full and the fruit is turning color, someone always asks permission to taste an olive. Another member of the group invariably blurts out that he or she should probably not do that, ruining my chance at a good schadenfreude moment.

Occasionally, folks will pluck an olive, and the look on their faces tells the tale of the unadulterated power of this remarkable, diminutive fruit. I often wonder how certain food traditions evolved, especially when something spectacular is coaxed out of something that on first blush is rather insipid. Even more confounding is the realization that for the first few thousand years when humans were producing olive oil, it was used for purposes other than cooking (lamp oil, cosmetics, etc.). It must have been an industrious or down-trodden individual who decided to cook up the day's harvest and make face cream.

Olives are one of the few things we grow, along with wine grapes, that do not go exclusively and immediately into the kitchen. John, Mike, and Fiorella use a certain amount of them, but for the most part the grapes go to the winery and our Manzanillo olives travel to a nearby facility to be pressed into our estate olive oil.

If you come for a tour of the farm or a meal or tasting at Edge, the gnarled olive trees will surely make an impression. There is no other tree that evokes the same feeling of connection to an ancient past in such an aesthetically pleasing way. And if you ask nicely when I'm showing you around the farm, I'll let you taste an olive. —*Colby*

LACTO-FERMENTED OLIVES

I was introduced to fermentation as a child by my Palestinian grandmother, who settled in Peru. She was an advocate of preserving as much food as she could and creating layers of flavor for her dishes. My many memories of the different spices and preserved vegetables she used are always an inspiration for my cooking. Living in a place where you have access to olive trees or a source for freshly harvested olives will give you the opportunity to try this recipe. —Fiorella

2 lb/1 kg freshly harvested, barely ripe green olives, such as Sevillano or Ascolano varieties

4 cups/1 l filtered water

½ cup/70 g kosher salt

2 tablespoons/28 ml apple cider vinegar

EQUIPMENT

2-qt /2-l widemouthed canning jar with lid and screw band

CHEF'S NOTE:

The green ripe olives called for in this recipe take longer to ferment than black ripe olives, such as the Manzanillo, Kalamata, Mission, and Botija varieties. To cure any of the black varieties, use freshly harvested ripe, but not overripe, olives and the same brine recipe, but after one week make a new batch of brine, drain the original brine from the jar, and replace it with the new brine. Let the olives ferment for 2 months, opening the jar every week to release carbon dioxide. Begin tasting the olives after 2 months, and once the bitterness is gone, drain the brine and cover the olives with extra-virgin olive oil and add flavorings of your preference, such as bay leaf, garlic, oregano, coriander, or citrus peel. Store the olives in the refrigerator for up to 1 year.

Wash the jar and lid in hot, soapy water. Rinse, then immerse the jar in gently boiling water for 10 minutes. Remove the jar from the hot water and shake off any excess. Have the lid and screw band ready.

Meanwhile, score each olive by making a small cut in it or by smashing it gently with a pestle or small wooden mallet. Put the olives in the sterilized jar. In a saucepan over medium heat, bring the water and salt to a boil, whisking to dissolve the salt. Set aside to cool to room temperature, then stir in the vinegar. Pour the cooled brine over the olives, making sure they are completely submerged in the liquid. If they are not submerged, they will spoil. Press gently on the olives with some plastic wrap, then cap the jar with the lid and twist on the screw band. Keep the jar in a dark place at around 65°F/18°C. The suggested temperature range for ferments is 60°F–68°F/15°C–20°C. If you live in a warm-weather area, check your ferments frequently because the process will be much faster in hotter climates. Once a week, remove the lid to release any built-up gases and then recap the jar.

Sample an olive every other week to check the bitterness level and to release carbon dioxide buildup. Be patient. The olives can be eaten when the strong bitterness is gone, which can take as long as 12 weeks. They should remain submerged the entire time to prevent mold from forming. If a white film develops on top, remove it by gently skimming the surface with a spoon. Replace the liquid with a little more brine, which can be prepared in the same way as above.

When the olives are ready, drain them, rinse them well with cool water, then flavor them as you like—with olive oil, garlic, chiles, citrus peel, herbs, or spices—using your creativity. Store them in an airtight container in the refrigerator for up to 1 year.

TUNA CONFIT IN AROMATIC OLIVE OIL

Having this tuna in the fridge, packed away in deliciously flavored olive oil, gives me peace of mind. I know I can pull some out for a quick and satisfying protein snack when my tank feels low or when I'm composing one of many Niçoise salad variations. All you need for a perfect summer supper is a generous piece of the tuna, a seven-minute boiled egg, good mayonnaise (preferably homemade), anchovies, olives, and a few tomatoes still warm from the sun. For the best sandwich imaginable, use these same ingredients to fill a split baguette.

Worldwide demand for tuna has taken a profound toll on populations of this versatile fish and has compromised the health of many tuna fisheries. In the Edge kitchen, we source all our fish conscientiously and look for hook-and-line-caught tuna from fisheries that we know are healthy. —Mike

---

1 lb/500 g best-quality albacore (tombo) or yellow fin (ahi) tuna steak, trimmed of any dark blood line

Artisanal sea salt

1 1/2 cups/375 ml extra-virgin olive oil

3 fresh thyme sprigs

3 very thin lemon slices

2 cloves garlic, smashed

A few tender fennel fronds

1/2 teaspoon pink peppercorns

1/2 teaspoon black peppercorns

1/4 teaspoon fennel seeds

Season the tuna steak generously with salt and set aside.

In a small pot with a diameter that will accommodate the tuna snugly, combine the olive oil, thyme, lemon slices, garlic, fennel fronds, pink and black peppercorns, and fennel seeds and heat over medium heat until the herbs just start to crackle and spatter in the oil. Turn off the heat and let the flavors infuse the oil for about 10 minutes.

Return the pot to the stove and warm over the lowest possible heat setting. I use a heat diffuser or cast-iron pan beneath the pot to keep the heat very low. Carefully slide the tuna into the oil. Let the tuna poach in the oil bath until the center of the steak starts to lose its raw color but is still pink and juicy, about 7 minutes.

Remove the pot from the heat and let the tuna cool to room temperature in the oil. Transfer the tuna to a container with an airtight lid, then strain the oil through a medium-mesh sieve held over the tuna. Cover with the lid and store in the refrigerator for up to 10 days.

This onion tart is a delicate riff on the traditional flatbread from the south of France, in which meltingly sweet onions contrast with briny olives and anchovies. Instead of the customary yeast dough, we use a flaky, buttery galette pastry. It's the same recipe we use for our fruit-based dessert tarts throughout the year. Pissaladière, served in small bites as a canapé along with a glass of Champagne, is our choice for welcoming guests to Edge. We also serve it as first course, cut into larger slices, alongside a garden lettuce salad with snipped herbs. If you want to get a head start on the recipe, make the dough and the onions the day before. —Mike

GALETTE PASTRY

2 cups/250 g all-purpose flour

1 teaspoon organic sugar

½ teaspoon artisanal sea salt

1½ cups/170 g chilled unsalted butter,
    cut into ½-inch/12-mm pieces,
    divided

½ cup/125 ml ice-cold water

¼ cup/60 ml extra-virgin olive oil

3 fresh thyme sprigs

1½ lb/750 g yellow onions, thinly sliced

Artisanal sea salt and freshly ground
    black pepper

1 large egg whisked with 1 teaspoon heavy
    cream for egg wash

10–12 olive oil–cured anchovy fillets,
    halved lengthwise

¼ cup/45 g Niçoise olives, pitted

To make the pastry dough, in a stand mixer fitted with the paddle attachment, combine the flour, sugar, and salt and mix briefly on medium speed until well blended. Add half the butter and continue to mix on medium speed until the butter pieces are the size of peas. With the mixer still on medium speed, add the remaining butter and mix just until this addition is in pieces the size of lima beans. On low speed, pulse the mixer on and off briefly while drizzling the water over the flour mixture until the dough has a rough, ropy consistency.

Lightly flour a work surface and turn the dough out onto it. Knead the dough once or twice just until it comes together somewhat cohesively. Resist the temptation to overmix the dough or the crust will turn out tough. Divide the dough in half, wrap each half in plastic wrap, and flatten the halves into disks about ½ inch/12 mm thick. Let rest in the refrigerator for at least 1 hour or up to 1 day. You will need only half the dough for this recipe. The other disk can be slipped into a lock-top plastic bag and frozen for up to 1 month; thaw overnight in the refrigerator.

Meanwhile, in a saucepan over medium heat, warm the olive oil. Toss in the thyme, and once it starts to crackle, add the onions. Season the onions with a generous pinch of salt and stir to mix well. Cover the pan, reduce the heat to medium-low, and cook, stirring often, until the onions are meltingly tender and sweet, about 30 minutes. Taste and season with a little more salt if needed and a few grinds of pepper. Remove from the heat and remove and discard the thyme sprigs.

Line a sheet pan with parchment paper. Spread the onions on the pan and let cool completely. The onions can be cooked a day in advance, cooled, and stored in an airtight container in the refrigerator.

Remove the dough from the refrigerator 10 minutes before rolling. Line a 13-by-18-inch/33-by-45-cm sheet pan with parchment paper, then lightly flour a work surface. Roll out the dough on the floured surface into an oval about 10 by 16 inches/25 by 40 cm. Trim off any uneven edges with a

paring knife or pizza cutter. Carefully transfer the dough
to the sheet pan and refrigerate for 30 minutes.

Preheat the oven to 400°F/200°C. Spread the onions
evenly over the dough, leaving a roughly 1 1/2-inch/4-cm
border uncovered. Fold the border over on itself and crimp
and flute the edge in any simple pattern around the onions.
Brush the edge with the egg wash.

Bake until lightly browned, about 15 minutes. Carefully
remove the galette from the oven and arrange the anchovy
fillets and olives in an attractive pattern on the onions.
Return to the oven until the crust turns a deep gold, about
10 minutes longer.

Let the galette cool on the pan over a wire rack for about
20 minutes, then cut into pieces and serve.

WARM OLIVES WITH PRESERVED LEMON

Cold olives right out of the refrigerator pale in comparison to ones brought to room temperature, especially after they have been basking in a marinade. Gently warming olives in a slow oven with aromatic herbs, garlic, and preserved lemon results in a slightly softer texture and takes the flavor a step further, imparting a deeper richness. This is an easy do-ahead dish for a dinner party or a complement to wine and cheese. —John

3 tablespoons extra-virgin olive oil

4 cloves garlic, halved lengthwise

½ teaspoon red pepper flakes

8 fresh thyme sprigs

1 preserved lemon (page 37), pulp discarded and peel rinsed and julienned or finely chopped

2 tablespoons dry white wine

1 lb/500 g brine-cured green olives, soaked in cold water for 30 minutes and drained

Preheat the oven to 350°F/180°C.

In a flameproof earthenware or other clay pot over medium-low heat, warm the olive oil. Add the garlic and cook, stirring occasionally, until softened, about 5 minutes. Add the pepper flakes, thyme, and preserved lemon and continue to cook, stirring occasionally, for 5 minutes longer. Add the wine and olives and stir and toss to mix well.

Cover, transfer to the oven, and bake for 20 minutes; the olives will soften slightly. Remove from the oven, uncover, and let cool for 10 minutes, then transfer to a bowl and serve warm.

Olives have always been part of breakfast at my house. My favorite are Botija olives, which are black olives picked ripe, kept raw, and lacto-fermented. If you are not able to find them, you can substitute Kalamata olives in this recipe. The tanginess and acidity of the sauce goes well with other seafood and vegetable dishes. Fresh whole calamari is preferable, but if they are not available, the already cleaned and recipe-ready product will suffice. —Fiorella

---

OLIVE SAUCE

½ cup/80 g pitted Lacto-Fermented Olives (page 201)

1 large egg yolk

1 serrano or other chile, seeds and membranes removed and finely chopped

½ teaspoon minced shallot

¼ teaspoon grated garlic

1 cup/250 ml extra-virgin olive oil

2 tablespoons fresh lime juice

Artisanal sea salt and freshly ground black pepper

½ lb/250 g fresh calamari or squid

Artisanal sea salt and freshly ground black pepper

1 tablespoon rendered duck fat

1 tablespoon fresh cilantro leaves

To make the sauce, combine the olives, egg yolk, chile, shallot, and garlic in a blender and process on low speed until smooth. With the motor running, slowly add the olive oil in a thin stream and process until fully incorporated. Finish with the lime juice and season to taste with salt and pepper. Transfer to a small bowl, cover, and reserve at room temperature if serving within 30 minutes; refrigerate if keeping longer.

To clean the calamari, working with one at a time, grasp the body in one hand and the head in the other and pull them apart. Cut off the tentacles straight down just behind the eyes and remove and discard the beak (the small, round cartilage piece connecting the tentacles to the head) from the tentacles. Squeezing the base of the tentacles is the easiest way to free it. Set the tentacles aside. Pull the quill-like cuttlebone from the body with your fingers and discard. With the back of a knife, and working from the closed end, gently press along the length of the body to force out any residual innards. Clean the remaining calamari the same way. Cut the bodies crosswise into rings about ½ inch/12 mm wide.

Heat a large sauté pan over medium-high. Season the calamari with salt and pepper. When the pan is hot, add the duck fat and the calamari and sauté just until opaque and fork-tender, 2–3 minutes. Be careful not to overcook the calamari or it will be chewy.

To serve, spoon some of the olive sauce on each plate. Add some calamari and garnish each serving with cilantro.

Asparagus, Olive, Fava Bean, Pickled Radish, and Tuna Salad

I am always excited to welcome the extra sunlight and beautiful produce that springtime brings. I feel inspired when I see the first asparagus come up at the farm, followed by a bounty of fava beans. This salad combines these two early-spring favorites with tuna confit. The radishes contribute some spiciness and acidity. —Fiorella

20 asparagus spears

Kosher salt

1 1/2 lb/750 g fava beans in their pods, shucked

3 Pickled Radishes (page 22)

5 tablespoons/80 ml extra-virgin olive oil

2 tablespoons fresh lemon or lime juice

Artisanal sea salt and freshly ground black pepper

3/4 lb/375 g Tuna Confit in Aromatic Olive Oil (page 205), cut into 12 equal pieces

1/2 cup/80 g pitted Kalamata olives, halved

2 tablespoons Olive Crumbles (page 202)

1 tablespoon torn fresh tarragon leaves

1 tablespoon cut-up fresh chives, in 1-inch/2.5-cm lengths

Cut off and discard the tough end from each asparagus spear, then halve each spear on the diagonal. Fill a large bowl with water and ice. Bring a saucepan filled with water to a rapid boil and salt generously with kosher salt. Add the asparagus and boil until crisp-tender, 2–3 minutes; the timing will depend on the thickness of the spears. With a spider or wire skimmer, scoop out the asparagus pieces and plunge them into the ice water bath until chilled. Scoop out the asparagus, drain well, and set aside.

Return the pan of water to a rapid boil and refresh the ice water bath with additional ice. Add the fava beans to the boiling water and boil just until tender, 2–3 minutes. Scoop out the beans and plunge them into the ice water bath until chilled. Drain well and peel away the tough outer skin from each bean.

Using a mandoline, thinly slice the radishes lengthwise.

In a small bowl, whisk together the olive oil and lemon juice and season with salt and pepper to make a dressing. In a bowl, combine the asparagus and favas and coat lightly with some of the dressing.

To serve, arrange 3 pieces of tuna in the middle of each plate and place some favas, asparagus, and olives around the tuna pieces. Tuck the radishes in among the other vegetables. Drizzle each serving with a little dressing, then sprinkle some of the olive crumbles, tarragon, and chives around each one.

Braised Lamb with Moroccan Spices and Green Olives   SERVES 4–6

The green olives and spices in this recipe bring to mind travels in North Africa. Blending the spices and seasoning the meat a day before cooking, though not essential, deepens the flavor and helps ensure a more succulent dish. After several hours in the oven, this lamb is fork-tender and virtually makes its own aromatic sauce. The principles of braising are the same for any kind of meat, and mastering this method is within reach of all cooks. Serve this dish with couscous or rice. —John

---

Moroccan Spice Blend

2 teaspoons coriander seeds

2 teaspoons cumin seeds

Large pinch of saffron threads

½ teaspoon ground turmeric

½ teaspoon Fermented Red Pepper Powder (page 147) or other ground red pepper, such as piment d'Espelette or Aleppo

3½ lb/1.75 kg boneless lamb shoulder, trimmed of excess fat

1 tablespoon artisanal sea salt

Freshly ground black pepper

2 tablespoons extra-virgin olive oil

2 yellow onions, coarsely chopped

4 cloves garlic, chopped

1 tablespoon peeled and grated fresh ginger

3 cups/750 ml chicken stock or water

1 cinnamon stick, preferably Ceylon, 3–4 inches/7.5–10 cm long

8 fresh cilantro stems, tied in a bundle

1 cup/180 g pit-in brine-cured green olives

1 Preserved Lemon (page 37), pulp discarded and peel rinsed and julienned or finely chopped

Steamed rice or couscous for serving

Equipment

Spice mill

Food mill (optional)

The day before cooking, make the spice mixture and season the lamb. In a spice mill, combine the coriander, cumin, and saffron and grind to a powder. Add the turmeric and red pepper and grind until well mixed.

Sprinkle the lamb on all sides with half the spice mixture, then season evenly with the salt and several grinds of pepper. Place on a rack in a pan and refrigerate uncovered overnight. Remove the lamb from the refrigerator and let stand at room temperature for 1–2 hours before cooking.

Preheat the oven to 400°F/200°C. Heat a heavy, flameproof roasting pan or enameled casserole large enough to accommodate the lamb over medium-high. Add the olive oil and then the onions, garlic, and ginger. Reduce the heat to medium-low and cook, stirring occasionally, until the onions and garlic have softened, about 10 minutes. Add the remaining spice mixture and cook for a few minutes, stirring occasionally, until aromatic. Add the stock, cinnamon stick, and cilantro bundle and raise the heat to medium-high, scraping the bottom of the pan to dislodge any browned-on bits. Set the lamb, fat side up, in the roasting pan, cover, and transfer it to the oven. Reduce the oven temperature to 325°F/165°C and cook the lamb for 1 hour. Remove the cover, turn the lamb over, and cook uncovered for 45 minutes. Turn the lamb one more time and cook, still uncovered, for an additional 45 minutes.

Carefully transfer the meat to a platter and allow to cool a bit before cutting. Discard the cinnamon stick and cilantro stems and pour the contents of the pan through a fine-mesh sieve into a saucepan, pressing lightly on the onions and garlic with the back of a spoon to release as much liquid as possible. (If you have a food mill, it is even better for this step.) Discard the onions and garlic.

Bring to a boil on the stove top, skimming the fat from the surface. Using a chef's knife, cut the lamb into serving-size chunks and return them to the roasting pan. Add the olives, preserved lemon, and hot liquid and then return the pan to the oven and continue to cook until the meat is fork-tender, about 30 minutes. Check the lamb for doneness by inserting a fork and gently twisting it. It should rotate easily. Remove from the oven and let rest for 15 minutes. Serve the lamb with the pan sauce spooned over it.

CHOCOLATE AND OLIVE OIL MOUSSE

SERVES 6

It may seem like we are stretching the boundaries of dessert by adding olive oil here, but it actually makes sense for us. We grow olives and produce our own oil, so why shouldn't we use it liberally? Olive oil ice cream is a staple in our kitchen, as is olive oil cake with strawberries steeped in vanilla and olive oil. For the mousse, use a high-quality fruity olive oil with medium pungency and moderate bitterness, such as ours, made from Manzanillo olives. —John

---

6 oz/185 g bittersweet chocolate (such as Valrhona or Callebaut, 70 percent cacao), coarsely chopped, plus shavings for garnish

¼ cup/60 ml extra-virgin olive oil

3 large eggs, separated

4 tablespoons/50 g organic sugar, divided

Artisanal sea salt

1 cup/240 ml heavy cream

1 teaspoon pure vanilla extract

Fill a saucepan half full with water and bring the water to a bare simmer. Put the chocolate and olive oil in a heatproof bowl, rest the bowl in the saucepan over (not touching) the water, and immediately turn off the heat. The residual heat will be enough to melt the chocolate gently. Let cool to room temperature, remove the bowl from the pan, and stir to blend the chocolate and oil.

Bring the water back to a bare simmer. In a separate heatproof bowl, combine the egg yolks and 3 tablespoons of the sugar, place over (not touching) the water, and whisk constantly. After a minute or so, the yolks will be pale and thick. Remove from the saucepan and continue to whisk until cooled, about 2 minutes. Whisk the cooled yolk mixture into the melted chocolate mixture.

In a clean bowl, using a clean whip attachment or beaters, mix together the egg whites and a pinch of salt on medium speed until foamy. Continue beating until the egg whites begin to hold their shape. Add the remaining 1 tablespoon sugar, increase the speed to medium-high, and beat until the egg whites are thick and shiny and just hold a soft peak. Do not overbeat. Set aside.

In a clean bowl, using a clean whip attachment or beaters or a whisk, whip the cream with the vanilla until it holds a soft peak.

Make sure that everything—the chocolate and egg yolk mixture, the egg whites, and the whipped cream—is at room temperature before proceeding to the next step. Fold one-third of the beaten egg whites into the chocolate mixture to lighten it, then gently fold in the remaining egg whites just until incorporated. Last, fold one-third of the whipped cream into the chocolate–egg white mixture to lighten it, then gently fold in the remaining whipped cream just until no white streaks remain.

Spoon the mousse into small glass dessert bowls or wineglasses, cover with plastic wrap, and chill for several hours. Just before serving, top each portion with chocolate shavings and a pinch of salt.

GRAPES

I SUPPOSE YOU COULD SAY THAT CRUSHING, pressing, fermenting, and bottling grapes ranks as the ultimate preservation project. Grapes are the only fruit grown by Stone Edge Farm that we do not preserve on the premises at Edge. Our winemaker, Jeff Baker, works his fermenting magic at our modern winery, only minutes away from our location in downtown Sonoma.

The heady aromas of spices, black pepper, and chocolate, mingled with the taste of dark fruits, make Jeff's Cabernet Sauvignons a joy to pair with food. Wine is neither just a beverage nor exactly a food, though it is sometimes described as one because of the many flavors in a single sip.

RECICPES

VERJUS 225

OVEN-DRIED GRAPES 225

SABA 226

SALAD WITH COOKED AND RAW VEGETABLES,
AUTUMN GREENS, AND
SABA-VERJUS DRESSING 228

HALIBUT COOKED IN GRAPE LEAVES
WITH GRAPES AND ALMONDS 231

HERB-CRUSTED FILLET OF BEEF WITH
RED WINE JUS 232

DUCK LEGS WITH SABA, GRAPES, AND
CULTURED POLENTA 237

CABERNET SAUVIGNON GRAPE AND
WINE GRANITA 241

It is more like a fermented condiment that can elevate a meal. Many wines, especially white wines and lighter reds, need only a corkscrew and a glass to be enjoyed, but a brawny Cabernet Sauvignon demands something savory to be fully appreciated. A good wine is enhanced by food, balances food, and is even ennobled by food.

The whole grapevine is put to use in our kitchen. When vineyards are replanted, the underperforming vines are uprooted and removed; this presents us with a bonanza of woody trunks that, when cut to the proper size and seasoned, make a first-rate grilling fuel. Wrapping food in green grape leaves creates a wonderful protective package to keep things moist during grilling and roasting, and imparts a slightly sour tanginess. Ripe grapes of any kind—table or wine, cooked or raw—give a dish an intense burst of flavor and texture.

Midway through the growing season, when the immature Cabernet Sauvignon grapes begin to turn from green to blush, some clusters are harvested and pressed into a juice. This verjus, as it is called, is used in salad dressings and sauces when a gentle acidity is needed. At the end of harvest, a few clusters of grapes ready to be turned into wine are likewise diverted to the kitchen. These we cook down to make saba, a syrup with a complex sweet and tannic flavor. The richness of saba boosts a salad dressing or cheese plate and complements many dishes, notably duck and quail.

Wine, with all its nuanced flavors and aromas, has a way of moving to the front of our pantry shelves and, like our olive oil, finds its way into many different preparations. Long before we reach for a Stone Edge Farm Cabernet Sauvignon, the wine has been alive in the bottle, changing and shifting on a journey to its full, mature expression of self. —*John*

Verjus

Just before our Cabernet Sauvignon and Merlot grapes turn from green to the first blush of pink and purple, a stage called veraison, it's time to harvest some of the unripe clusters for processing into verjus—"green juice" in French. Its uses in cooking are many. With its soft acidity, compared to that of lemon juice or vinegar, verjus works well in a dressing for a salad that will pair beautifully with wine. —John

10 lb/5 kg green (unripe) red or white wine grapes, harvested just before veraison

EQUIPMENT

Four 1-qt/1-l glass jars with lids

Electric juicer or food mill

Rinse and air-dry the grape clusters, removing as much of the stem as possible. If an electric juicer is available, it will be the easiest method for extracting the juice. Alternatively, place the grape clusters in a big pot and, using a large, well-cleaned, unopened can of food, smash the grapes with abandon. Using a food mill fitted with the coarse disk, press the smashed grapes, then pass the juice through a fine-mesh sieve.

Wash 2 of the jars and lids in hot, soapy water. Rinse, then immerse the jars in gently boiling water for 10 minutes. Remove the jars from the hot water and shake off any excess. Pour the juice into the jars and cap tightly with the lids. Refrigerate for 48 hours to allow the sediment to settle.

Wash, rinse, and sterilize the remaining 2 jars and lids as before. Being careful not to disturb the sediment in the first 2 jars, pour the juice into the freshly sterilized jars. (This is called racking.) Cap the jars and refrigerate. The verjus will keep for 2–3 months.

Oven-Dried Grapes

Oven-drying grapes intensifies and sweetens their flavor but keeps them more like grapes than raisins. We use these on cheese plates and in autumn salads. —John

1 lb/500 g seedless red grapes

Preheat the oven to 200°F/95°C. Line a sheet pan with parchment paper.

Rinse and air-dry the grapes, then remove them from their stems. Cut the grapes in half and arrange, cut sides up, in a snug single layer on the pan. Bake until wrinkled and half their original size, about 3 hours.

Let cool, transfer to a jar, cap tightly, and store in the refrigerator for up to 1 week.

Saba

Saba, or mosto cotto *(cooked grape must) in Italian, is an essential part of cooking at Edge. It adds acidity and a grapey sweetness to many of our dishes. Every harvest, we make our own saba by gleaning ripe grape bunches from our Cabernet Sauvignon vineyard and boiling them in large pots over an open fire. For this recipe, however, we have moved the cooking indoors. After the grapes have released their juice, the must is strained and further reduced to a syrup. We have tried this without success using table grapes, so if you are going to do it right, source some wine grapes. —John*

---

10 lb/5 kg red wine grapes

Equipment

Chinois (fine-mesh conical sieve)

1-pt/500-ml canning jar with lid and
  screw band

Cheesecloth

Jar tongs

Put the grapes, stems and all, in a large, heavy pot and cover it. Place the pot over medium-low on the stove top and heat slowly to avoid scorching. When the grapes begin to soften and their juice is flowing, uncover the pot and raise the heat. Boil very gently for 30 minutes, stirring occasionally as the grapes release all their juice.

Remove the pot from the heat and pass the grapes through a chinois into another pot or a bowl, using the bottom of a ladle to push through as much juice as possible. Clean the cooking pot, pour the strained juice back into it, and return it to a low boil. Boil the juice until it is reduced by two-thirds. This step will take at least 1 hour and requires your undivided attention to ensure the pot does not boil over. The juice will be quite thick—the consistency of maple syrup. Remove from the heat.

Meanwhile, wash the jar and lid in hot, soapy water. Rinse, then immerse the jar in gently boiling water for 10 minutes. Remove the jar from the hot water and shake off any excess. Have the lid and screw band ready.

Pour the reduced juice through cheesecloth into the jar, leaving ½-inch/12-mm headspace, and wipe any spills from the rim with a damp towel. Cap the jar with the lid and twist on the screw band, tightening gently with just your fingertips.

Place a wire rack in the bottom of a saucepan and set the jar on the rack. Fill the pan with water, covering the jar by about 3 inches/7.5 cm. Cover the pan, bring the water to a boil over high heat, and boil for 15 minutes.

Using the jar tongs, transfer the jar to a work surface and let cool completely. Then check for a good seal by loosening the screw band and pressing on the center of the lid. If it remains concave and does not move, the seal is good. Store the jar in a cool, dark place for up to 1 year. If the jar failed to seal properly, store in the refrigerator and use the saba within 3 months.

Verjus (left) and saba (right)

Salad with Cooked and Raw Vegetables, Autumn Greens, and Saba-Verjus Dressing

SERVES 4 TO 6

One of the things I am most grateful for as a cook in California is the variety of produce that each season brings. As the grapes in our vineyards ripen, it is an ongoing project in our kitchen to make verjus and saba. The dressing for this recipe uses both. I use a combination of raw and cooked veggies to create a hearty fresh salad. It can be served family-style on a large platter. —Fiorella

---

12 small beets, any color, tops removed

2½ tablespoons plus 1 teaspoon expeller-pressed avocado oil, divided

Artisanal sea salt and freshly ground black pepper

2 fresh thyme sprigs, divided

2 shallots, unpeeled

5 carrots, peeled and chopped

1 small bunch celery, leaves removed and reserved for garnish

1 teaspoon Verjus (page 225)

1 small Delicata squash, halved lengthwise, seeded, and cut crosswise into slices ½ inch/12 mm thick

Saba-Verjus Dressing

½ cup/125 ml extra-virgin olive oil

Reserved shallot paste

2 tablespoons Saba (page 226)

2 tablespoons Verjus (page 225)

Artisanal sea salt and freshly ground black pepper

1 head radicchio, leaves separated, then halved horizontally into bite-size pieces

6 baby carrots, thinly sliced lengthwise with a mandoline

¼ cup/40 g pumpkin seeds, toasted

¼ cup/35 g Oven-Dried Grapes (page 225)

Equipment

Mortar and pestle (optional)

Preheat the oven to 375°F/190°C. Put the beets in a small roasting pan with 3 tablespoons of water. Drizzle with 1 tablespoon of the avocado oil, and season with salt, pepper, and 1 thyme sprig. Cover with aluminum foil or a lid and roast until tender when pierced, 30–40 minutes, depending on the size of the beets. Let cool, then peel, cut in half lengthwise, and set aside.

Place the shallots in a small roasting pan or cast-iron frying pan, drizzle with 1 teaspoon of the avocado oil, and season with salt and pepper. Roast in the oven until soft to the touch, about 30 minutes. Let cool, peel, and crush to a paste in the mortar with the pestle or with the back of a chef's knife on a cutting board. Reserve for the dressing.

In a small saucepan over medium heat, combine the carrots, water to cover, the remaining thyme sprig, ½ teaspoon salt, and ¼ teaspoon pepper and bring to a simmer. Cover and cook until the carrots are tender, 15–20 minutes. Remove from the heat and drain into a fine-mesh sieve placed over a bowl. Remove and discard the thyme sprig, then transfer the carrots to a blender or food processor and purée, using some of the reserved cooking liquid if needed to achieve a smooth consistency. Pass the purée through the sieve, pressing against it with the back of a spoon or a rubber spatula. Keep warm and reserve.

Separate the celery ribs, then peel them and cut them crosswise on the diagonal into pieces 1 inch/2.5 cm long. In a small sauté pan over low heat, warm the verjus. Add the celery and cook, stirring occasionally, until tender with a slight crunch, about 5 minutes. Season with salt and pepper, remove from the heat, and reserve.

In a large cast-iron frying pan over medium-high heat, warm the remaining 1½ tablespoons avocado oil. Add the squash slices and sear on both sides until tender and golden brown, 5–10 minutes. Season with salt and pepper and reserve.

To make the dressing, gently whisk together the olive oil, shallot paste, saba, and verjus in a small bowl. Season with salt and pepper.

In a bowl, combine the radicchio and sliced raw carrots, drizzle with a little of the dressing, and toss to coat lightly.

To assemble, place a heaping spoonful of the carrot purée on each plate and arrange 3 beets, some celery, and some radicchio and raw carrots over and around the purée. Finish with the squash and garnish with the pumpkin seeds and grapes.

HALIBUT COOKED IN GRAPE LEAVES WITH GRAPES AND ALMONDS   SERVES 4

Wrapping ingredients with grapes leaves, a technique I learned from my grandmother, is a great way to add flavor. In this recipe, the leaves allow the fish to steam, keeping it moist and giving it a pleasantly sour taste. You can serve this with rice, potatoes, salad, or any other side dish that you love. —Fiorella

1 teaspoon cardamom seeds

1 teaspoon coriander seeds

4 allspice berries

4 skinless halibut or other firm white fish
   fillets, each 5 oz/155 g and
   1 inch/2.5 cm thick

Artisanal sea salt and freshly ground
   black pepper

1 lemon, cut crosswise into slices
   1/2 inch/12 mm thick (4 slices total)

4 cloves garlic, thinly sliced

12–16 large fresh or jarred grape leaves

4 tablespoons/60 ml extra-virgin olive
   oil, divided

3/4 cup/180 ml dry white wine, divided

1 small bunch fresh thyme
   (about 16 sprigs), divided

2 bay leaves, divided

1 shallot, minced

7 tablespoons/105 g unsalted butter,
   cut into small pieces

1/4 cup/60 g whole almonds, blanched,
   peeled, and toasted

1/4 lb/125 g seedless green grapes, peeled

EQUIPMENT
Spice mill

In a small cast-iron frying pan over low heat, toast the cardamom, coriander, and allspice, shaking the pan occasionally, until fragrant, 3–4 minutes. Pour into the spice mill, let cool, grind finely, and reserve.

Preheat the oven to 300°F/150°C. Season the fish on both sides with salt, pepper, and the ground spices. Put a lemon slice and one-fourth of the garlic slices on top of each piece of fish. If using fresh grape leaves, remove the stems from the leaves, blanch the leaves in boiling water for 30 seconds, then refresh in ice water, drain well on paper towels, and blot dry. If using jarred leaves, rinse them under cold running water and pat dry. Overlap 3 or 4 leaves, stem side up, to create a circular pattern. Set a fish piece on top and gently fold the leaves into a neat packet. Repeat with the remaining leaves and fish pieces.

In a roasting pan just large enough to accommodate the fish packets, combine 2 tablespoons of the olive oil, 1/2 cup/120 ml of the wine, half of the thyme, and 1 of the bay leaves. Gently place the fish packets on top and bake for 15–20 minutes; the timing will depend on the thickness of the fillets. Remove from the oven, flip each package over in the pan, and set aside in a warm place.

To make the sauce, in a small sauté pan over medium heat, combine the remaining 2 tablespoons olive oil and the shallot and sauté until the shallot is softened, about 2 minutes. Add the remaining thyme and the remaining bay leaf and sauté until fragrant, about 30 seconds. Add the remaining 1/4 cup/60 ml wine and cook until reduced by three-fourths, about 3 minutes. Add the butter pieces and whisk constantly until fully emulsified. Remove from the heat, pass through a fine-mesh sieve set over a small bowl, and add the almonds and the grapes. Season with salt and pepper.

To serve, place the fish packets on plates, unwrap the grape leaves to reveal the fish, and spoon some sauce over each portion, dividing the grapes and almonds evenly.

Herb-Crusted Fillet of Beef with Red Wine Jus

SERVES 4–6

Filet mignon is generally not the chef's first choice. We tend to like cuts with more character, such as hanger, flat iron, and tri-tip. But the tenderloin has one thing going for it if cooked correctly, which is a sublime texture. The issue that chefs have with beef tenderloin is that its flavor is on the bland side. That's because this cut has no fat or marbling. Here, the beef is encased in a blanket of fresh herbs and spices that boosts the flavor, and a beefy red wine sauce adds needed depth. A crispy Potato Rösti (page 119) is the perfect accompaniment. —John

---

2 lb/1 kg center-cut beef tenderloin

2 teaspoons artisanal sea salt

2 teaspoons freshly ground black pepper

1 tablespoon juniper berries

4 cloves garlic

²/₃ cup/30 g chopped fresh flat-leaf parsley, thyme, rosemary, mint, and basil, in equal amounts

1 tablespoon extra-virgin olive oil

Red Wine Sauce

3 teaspoons expeller-pressed grapeseed oil or rendered duck fat, divided

1 lb/500 g boneless beef chuck, cut into small dice

1 yellow onion, finely chopped

1 carrot, peeled and finely chopped

1 small celery root, peeled and finely chopped

2 cups/500 ml Cabernet Sauvignon or other full-bodied red wine

Several fresh thyme sprigs

1 bay leaf

3 cups/750 ml rich beef or chicken stock

Artisanal sea salt and freshly ground pepper

Potato Rösti (page 119) for serving

Equipment

Mortar and pestle (optional)

Instant-read thermometer

Begin this dish 24 hours before serving. Trim the tenderloin of all fat and silver skin and season with the salt and pepper. Using the mortar and pestle, pound the juniper berries and garlic to a rough paste. Finely chop together all the herbs, add to the juniper-garlic paste along with the olive oil, and pound together until well mixed, about 1 minute. If you do not have a mortar and pestle, finely chop the juniper berries and garlic, then transfer to a food processor, add the herbs and olive oil, and pulse until a rough paste forms, being careful to not overprocess. Evenly press the mixture onto the meat. As you work, some will fall off, so just keep re-pressing until it all sticks. Set a wire rack on a sheet pan, place the tenderloin on the rack, cover loosely with aluminum foil, and refrigerate.

The next day, remove the meat from the refrigerator 2 hours before roasting and allow to rest uncovered at room temperature.

To make the sauce, in a rondeau (brazier) or other large, wide, shallow pan over medium heat, warm 2 teaspoons of the grapeseed oil. Add the beef chuck and cook, stirring frequently, until well browned, about 8 minutes. Pour the meat and any accumulated juices into a bowl.

Drizzle the remaining 1 teaspoon oil into the pan and reduce the heat to low. Add the onion, carrot, and celery root and cook, stirring frequently, just until well browned, 25–30 minutes. Return the meat and its juices to the pan, add the wine, thyme, and bay leaf, and raise the heat to medium-high. Bring to a boil, reduce the heat to medium, and simmer until most of the wine has evaporated, about 15 minutes. Add the stock and return to a boil over medium-high heat. Lower the heat to a gentle simmer and begin reducing the sauce, skimming the fat off the surface with a large spoon or ladle as it appears. When the sauce has reduced by two-thirds, after about 35 minutes, remove it from the heat and pass it through a fine-mesh sieve held over a small saucepan. Season with salt and pepper. When ready to serve, gently reheat.

(continued)

Preheat the oven to 425°F/220°C. The tenderloin is
ideally roasted on a rack set on a sheet pan or roasting pan.
If this setup is not available, the meat can be successfully
roasted without a rack in a cast-iron, enameled-cast-iron,
or other thick-gauge pan.

Roast the tenderloin for 10 minutes. Turn it over and
continue roasting for 10 minutes longer. At this point,
using an instant-read thermometer, begin checking the
temperature every few minutes until it reaches an internal
temperature of 130°F/54°C for medium-rare. Remove
from the oven, transfer to a platter, and let rest for
10–15 minutes before cutting into slices 3/8 inch/1 cm thick.

To serve, place a wedge of the rösti on each plate. Lay
2 slices of the fillet next to the rösti and drizzle the sauce
over them.

Duck Legs with Saba, Grapes, and Cultured Polenta

SERVES 6

To celebrate the fruit of our vines at harvest, we cook duck legs in red wine and saba, the two capturing the lushness of fully ripened Cabernet Sauvignon and Merlot grapes. A small amount of buttermilk or natural yogurt lends its lactobacillus culture to polenta here, giving it a delicate tang and enhancing its creaminess. But you need time for this magic to happen. I inoculate the polenta before bedtime and cook it the next day. —Mike

---

POLENTA

1½ cups/250 g polenta (coarse-ground cornmeal)

5 cups/1.25 l filtered water, divided

1 tablespoon plain yogurt or buttermilk

1¼ teaspoons artisanal sea salt

4 tablespoons/60 g unsalted butter

½ cup/60 g freshly grated Parmesan cheese

DUCK LEGS

6 duck legs, 8–9 oz/250–280 g each, trimmed of excess fat

Artisanal sea salt and freshly ground black pepper

2 tablespoons Cognac or brandy

¼ lb/125 g bacon

6–7 fresh thyme sprigs, divided

4 fresh sage leaves

7 oz/220 g shallots, sliced

1½ cups/375 ml Cabernet Sauvignon or other full-bodied red wine

4 tablespoons/60 ml Saba (page 226), divided

6 cloves garlic, unpeeled, halved

1 cup/250 ml chicken stock, heated

1 large cluster wine or full-flavored table grapes, about ½ lb/250 g, snipped into several small clusters

The night before you plan to cook the polenta, combine the polenta, 1½ cups/375 ml of the water, and the yogurt or buttermilk in a small bowl and stir to mix well. Cover with plastic wrap and set aside in a draft-free place.

The next day, prepare the duck. Preheat the oven to 300°F/150°C. Generously season the duck legs with salt and pepper and drizzle evenly with the Cognac. In a saucepan over medium heat, cook the bacon until some of its fat has rendered and the bacon is lightly browned, about 5 minutes. Pour off and reserve about 1 tablespoon fat for the grapes. Toss 4 of the thyme sprigs, the sage, and the shallots into the pan and continue to cook over medium heat, stirring often, until the shallots have softened, about 5 minutes. Pour the wine and 2 tablespoons of the saba over the shallot mixture and bring to a boil. Reduce the heat to a simmer and cook until the liquid has reduced by about half, 8–10 minutes.

Remove from the heat and pour into a shallow baking dish that will accommodate the duck legs snugly in a single layer. Add the garlic to the dish, then arrange the duck legs, skin side down, in the dish. Pour the stock over the legs. Cover the dish with aluminum foil.

Bake for 45 minutes. Remove the foil and use tongs to turn the duck legs over, working carefully to avoid puncturing the skin. Return the duck to the oven and cook, uncovered, until the skin is dark golden brown, 30–45 minutes. Remove from the oven and let the duck legs cool in the baking dish. Transfer the cooled legs to a sheet pan and set aside for reheating prior to serving.

Discard the garlic cloves from the dish. Pour the contents of the baking dish through a fine-mesh sieve held over a bowl, pressing against the contents of the sieve with a rubber spatula or the back of a spoon to extract as much flavor as possible. Using a small ladle, skim off and discard the fat that rises to the surface of the braising juices. Reserve the juices.

(continued)

While the duck legs braise, whisk together the cultured polenta, the remaining 3½ cups/875 ml water, and the salt in a saucepan. Place over medium heat and bring to a simmer, whisking constantly as the polenta thickens. Reduce the heat to low and cover the pan so the polenta bubbles gently. Cook, stirring frequently with a wooden spoon, until the texture is creamy and the polenta tastes cooked, about 30 minutes. Remove from the heat and stir in the butter and cheese. Taste and adjust the seasoning with salt if needed. Keep covered in a warm spot.

Once the duck has cooled, and about 20 minutes before serving, raise the oven temperature to 400°F/200°C. In the same baking dish you used to cook the duck legs, toss the grape clusters with the remaining 2–3 thyme sprigs, the reserved 1 tablespoon bacon fat, the remaining 2 tablespoons saba, and a sprinkling of salt and pepper. Roast, basting a couple of times with the pan juices, until the grapes soften and start to split, about 10 minutes.

To serve, briefly warm the duck legs in the 400°F/200°C oven. At the same time, in a small saucepan, bring the reserved braising juices just to a boil. Spoon the polenta into a large serving bowl and top with the duck legs, or spoon the polenta into individual serving bowls and top each serving with a duck leg. Drizzle some of the braising juices around the duck and garnish with the roasted grapes.

CABERNET SAUVIGNON GRAPE AND WINE GRANITA

MAKES 4 1/2 CUPS/1.1 L; SERVES 6–8

For this recipe it is essential to use grapes with character, which would include wine grapes and exclude the garden–variety types from the supermarket. Here, I use a mixture of Concord and Cabernet Sauvignon grapes that are only days away from harvest. The seeds and stems contain a lot of flavor, so I run the grapes through a juicer and then cook the juice with the seeds, stems, and pulp. Alternatively, the grapes can be smashed vigorously with a potato masher in a pot before continuing. To serve, add a scoop of vanilla ice cream or sweetened whipped cream, if desired. —John

3 lb/1.5 kg mixed Concord and wine grapes (if available) with seeds

1/2 cup/125 ml water

2 cups/500 ml Cabernet Sauvignon

1/2 cup/100 g organic sugar

Juice of 1/2 lemon

Saba (page 226) for serving

EQUIPMENT

Juicer (optional)

Place a 3-qt/3-l glass baking dish in the freezer.

If a juicer is available, process the grapes in the juicer, saving the pulp, seeds, and stems and reuniting them with the juice in a large saucepan. Alternatively, place the grape clusters in a large saucepan and, using a large, well-cleaned, unopened can of food, smash the grapes with abandon. Add the water, wine, and sugar and bring to a boil over medium heat. Reduce the heat to low and cook for 10 minutes.

Remove from the heat, let cool completely, and stir in the lemon juice. Pass the mixture through a fine-mesh sieve held over a bowl, using a rubber spatula, ladle, or the back of a spoon to press out as much liquid as possible.

Remove the baking dish from the freezer, pour in the grape liquid, and return the dish to the freezer. Check after 30 minutes. The liquid should be starting to freeze around the edges. Using a fork, scrape the icy crystals toward the unfrozen center, then return the dish to the freezer. Repeat every 30 minutes with the goal of scarifying the ice each time to break up any large chunks. It should take about 4 hours total. The granita is ready when the baking dish is filled with loose, fluffy crystals.

Scoop the granita into chilled glass goblets and drizzle each serving with a teaspoon of saba.

JOHN McREYNOLDS is the culinary director of Stone Edge Farm. He was previously the co-owner and founding chef of the acclaimed Cafe La Haye in Sonoma, California. His early interest in food and wine led him to the California Culinary Academy, in San Francisco, where he was awarded a scholarship sponsored by Julia and Paul Child. He has cooked professionally for a Colorado dude ranch, a hotel on a Norwegian fjord, a French restaurant on Lake Chiemsee in Germany, a yacht sailing the Mediterranean, and George Lucas's Skywalker Ranch. In 2013, his *Stone Edge Farm Cookbook* was named Book of the Year by the International Association of Culinary Professionals (IACP). For the same title, John also received IACP's 2013 Julia Child Award for Best First Book.

MIKE EMANUEL was born in Southern California during the advent of the free-spirited, seasonally inspired California-cuisine movement. After graduating from the Culinary Institute of America in Hyde Park, New York, he returned to his home state and worked in top San Francisco Bay Area kitchens before landing at Chez Panisse, in Berkeley. Working under Alice Waters, Mike honed his cooking skills and developed his palate. He has cooked as a chef and caterer for private clients and has traveled in northern Italy, France, the Basque Country, Vietnam, and Mexico to experience different cultures through their cuisines. As estate chef, he collaborates with John and Fiorella to expand the mission of generously and artfully bringing the bounty of Stone Edge Farm to the table for guests.

FIORELLA BUTRON'S creative, colorful approach to cooking and life reflect her Peruvian, Palestinian, Genoese, and Spanish roots. A graduate of Le Cordon Bleu in Lima, Peru, she worked at the city's La Rosa Nautica before continuing her culinary training in the United States, in the kitchens of the Four Seasons in Palm Beach and Maui, the Wailea Beach Marriott, and Jay Bistro in Fort Collins, Colorado. Her exploration of foods and cultures took her throughout Latin America and to Southeast Asia, Europe, the San Francisco Bay Area, and India before she made her home in Napa. She joined the kitchen at Stone Edge Farm in 2016 and is the chef de cuisine.

Visitor Resources

Visiting and Dining at Edge

Our private club, Edge, located a few steps from the Plaza in downtown Sonoma, California, is reserved primarily for Collectors Cellar members of Stone Edge Farm Winery. Several times a week, we also welcome nonmember guests. Please visit our website, www.stoneedgefarm.com, or email Larry Nadeau (larry@stoneedgefarm.com) to reserve your place at Edge for lunch, dinner, or a tasting of our estate-grown wines accompanied by paired selections from our kitchen.

Special arrangements can be made to host certain private events at Edge. To inquire about a reception, lunch, or dinner, please email Larry Nadeau (larry@stoneedgefarm.com) or call us at 707-935-6520.

To request a wine-tasting appointment, please go to the "Visit" page of our website, www.stoneedgefarm.com, or contact either our Director of Hospitality, Philippe Thibault (707-486-6083, philippe@stoneedgefarm.com) or our Director of Sales and Marketing, Dorothe Cicchetti (707-508-7327, dorothe@stoneedgefarm.com).

Purchasing Stone Edge Farm Cookbooks, Wine, and Olive Oil

Additional copies of *Stone Edge Farm Kitchen Larder Cookbook* can be ordered from www.rizzolibookstore.com or purchased in bookstores. Copies of *Stone Edge Farm Cookbook* can be ordered on the "Purchase" page of our website, www.stoneedgefarm.com, or by calling us at 707-935-6520. Requests to host a book talk and book signing by our author(s) at your venue may be sent to John McReynolds (john@stoneedgefarm.com). To request a private cooking demonstration at the Edge kitchen, please call us at 707-935-6520.

Stone Edge Farm wines are sold exclusively to our Collectors Cellar members and mailing list customers. To purchase wine, please visit the "Purchase" page on our website, www.stoneedgefarm.com. Our estate olive oil is also available in limited quantities.

For information about joining our Collectors Cellar family, please contact our Director of Membership, Frieda Guercio (frieda@stoneedgefarm.com).

We welcome your inquiries and sincerely appreciate your interest in our offerings.

ACKNOWLEDGMENTS

We thank, with profound gratitude …

Mac and Leslie McQuown, the proprietors of Stone Edge Farm, for creating a dynamic environment that encourages creativity and innovation in harmony with the natural world. The McQuowns are truly generous patrons and designers of change in the world as well as great collaborators with us at Edge and Stone Edge Farm Winery.

Leslie Sophia Lindell for telling the story of our food and wine so artfully through her gorgeous and enticing photographs.

Jennifer Barry, the architect of our vision, for her expert eye for details large and small, and endless patience in trying to herd three chefs toward the common goal of making a book that takes the reader behind the scenes at a modern winery kitchen.

Our editor, Jill Hunting, for her patient mentoring, steady influence, and abiding friendship. Jill helped us translate our thoughts into sentences and gently pushed each of us to express our unique voice and elevate our writing.

At Rizzoli, our publisher Charles Miers and editor Jono Jarrett for championing the book.

Our gardener, friend, and co-writer Colby Eierman for growing the fruits and vegetables that we transform in our kitchen and for contributing his perspective on gardening through his essays. Without the garden and Colby, there is no book.

Lynda Balslev for her skillful professional recipe testing, Sharon Silva for her meticulous fact-checking and copyediting, Eve Lynch for her excellent proofreading, and Ken DellaPenta for his reader-friendly indexing.

Ivan Castillo, who supports us in the kitchen, and Larry Nadeau for going easy on the schedule at Edge in the weeks when we were occupied with photo shoots and writing deadlines, and for running the dining room with grace, professionalism, and geniality.

Stone Edge Farm Kitchen Larder Cookbook
Seasonal Recipes for Pantry and Table

By John McReynolds, Mike Emanuel, and Fiorella Butron
Photographs by Leslie Sophia Lindell

First published in the United States of America in 2019
By Rizzoli International Publications, Inc.
300 Park Avenue South, New York, NY 10010
www.rizzoliusa.com

The Stone Edge Farm logo, the *Vine of Life*, embodies our principle to live and create while
honoring nature's cycle of life through sustainability, respect, and conservation.

2019 2020 2021 2022 / 10 9 8 7 6 5 4 3 2 1

Distributed in the U.S. trade by Random House, New York
Printed in China

ISBN-13: 978-0-8478-6454-6

Library of Congress Control Number: 2018951546

Produced and designed by Jennifer Barry Design, Fairfax, California
Editor: Jill Hunting
Design Assistant: Shelly Peppel
Recipe Testing: Lynda Balslev
Prop Styling: Glenn Jenkins
Copyediting: Sharon Silva